How to Spell Like a Champ

by Barrie Trinkle, Carolyn Andrews,
and Paige Kimble

WORKMAN PUBLISHING, NEW YORK

Library of Congress Cataloging-in-Publication Data is available.

ISBN-13: 978-0-7611-4369-7
ISBN-10: 0-7611-4369-6

Design by Barbara Balch
Illustrations by Robert Zimmerman

Workman books are available at special discounts when purchased in bulk for premiums and sales promotions as well as for fund-raising or educational use. Special editions or book excerpts can also be created to specification. For details, contact the Special Sales Director at the address below.

Workman Publishing Company, Inc.
225 Varick Street
New York, NY 10014-4381
www.workman.com

Printed in the U.S.A.

First printing October 2006

10 9 8 7 6 5 4 3 2 1

For all the kids who want
to spell every word right,
but especially for F-i-o-n-a
—B.T.

word with the same ancestor, still in use in modern English, is *boon,* meaning "a timely benefit or blessing.") In England, a dialectal form of this word, *been* or *bean,* referred to "voluntary help given by neighbors toward the accomplishment of a particular task" *(Webster's Third). Bee* may simply be a shortened form of *been,* but no one is entirely certain.

What Makes a Spelling Bee?

Not all spelling bees are alike; the difficulty of the words, the size of the audience, the rules, and the prizes vary widely. But all spelling bees, even written spelling bees, have a few essential elements: contestants, a word list, and a pronouncer who gives the words aloud. Most spelling bees also have judges who oversee the bee to make sure it is fair to all spellers.

A school spelling bee might choose one or two students to represent each class, or it might be open to all comers. Most often,

Noah Webster, the father of the American dictionary.

Spellbound, a quirky documentary about several participants in the 1999 National Spelling Bee finals, becomes an art-house hit and is nominated for an Academy Award.

The 25th Annual Putnam County Spelling Bee, adapted from the off-Broadway play *C-R-E-P-U-S-C-U-L-E,* becomes the first Broadway musical about you-know-what.

❝*Bene . . . boon . . . been . . . bean . . . bee!* **❞**

Bee Season hits the big screen, starring Richard Gere, Juliette Binoche, and Flora Cross.

Akeelah and the Bee, written and directed by Doug Atchison and starring Laurence Fishburne, Angela Bassett, and Keke Palmer, opens just before the National Spelling Bee finals.

American Bee: The National Spelling Bee and the Culture of Word Nerds by James Maguire is published.

a teacher or principal serves as the pronouncer. There could be a separate judge or judges, or it might be up to the pronouncer to make sure that all students are given a fair chance to spell correctly. Homeschooled students might compete individually in a school spelling bee near their home, or they might spell against other homeschoolers to produce one or more homeschooling champions for an area.

As a speller moves ahead, spelling competition gets more serious. A local spelling bee can be written, oral, or a combination of both. Many spellers prefer competing in written bees. Since they take less time, why aren't all spelling competitions written? Spelling bees are held only partly for their educational value. They are also community events, and let's face it: Watching a roomful of kids writing on pieces of paper can be a snooze. Local and regional

Victory of a school spelling bee.

Reason #9 to Enter a Spelling Bee: Classrooms that have 100 percent participation get to have pizza parties.

spelling bees that feed into the National Spelling Bee are usually sponsored by newspapers, and an oral spelling bee is more exciting and makes better news. If a regional bee is very large, there may be a written round before the oral finals just to winnow the field of contestants down to a number that will fit onstage.

Local and regional bees are usually a lot bigger than a school bee, although they may sometimes be held in a school auditorium. They can be a blast to watch! There are always parents and teachers in the audience, and so there is usually some entertainment. Often, a master of ceremonies gives a funny or interesting presentation before the spelling starts. Sometimes there are free cookies. Soon, though, everyone turns to the matter at hand: determining a champion (or sometimes multiple champions) who will represent the area at a larger bee, perhaps at the National Spelling Bee.

Top Ten Reasons to Enter a Spelling Bee

10. There's an off-chance they'll make a movie about me.

9. Classrooms that have 100 percent participation get to have pizza parties.

8. Want to impress a geeky heartthrob in chem class.

7. My class will get an extra field trip.

6. Want to humiliate a really annoying classmate.

5. Need the trophy to keep my unmatched socks in.

4. Need a new dictionary.

3. Could use the T-shirt.

2. Will do anything to get out of class for an hour.

1. Mom is making me do it.

In 1925, the first national champion won $500 in $20 gold pieces.

Bee There

Most local spelling bees are open to the public. If you want to attend one near your home, contact your area's sponsoring newspaper to find out when and where its local or regional competition takes place. Direct your inquiry to the "spelling bee coordinator."

The National Spelling Bee finals are not open to the public; there simply isn't a room in Washington, D.C., big enough to hold all who would like to attend it. Media representatives need space for their equipment and a clear view of the contestants, and the finalists' families and friends take up the rest of the available seats. But the National Spelling Bee is always televised, so it's available to an audience of millions and is often rebroadcast again and again.

Of course, one of the best ways to see a spelling bee is from the stage—as a participant.

These bees typically have a more experienced pronouncer than school bees do. They also have one or more judges who pay careful attention to each contestant's spelling, determining whether the word has been spelled correctly. The judges also handle formal protests about the fairness of a speller's elimination and may reinstate a speller if they decide that it is the right thing to do, according to the rules of their contest.

The path to the National Spelling Bee is not the same for everyone. Some sponsoring newspapers are small, with a subscriber base that covers only one county, so some spellers win a school bee, then a county spelling title, and go from there straight to the national finals in Washington, D.C. Others must win or be in the top group of finishers in a county bee and then win a regional bee that covers multiple counties or even an entire state. At the national finals, contestants who represent a large area often arrive very well prepared, having competed several times over a few months— but that doesn't guarantee them a spot at the top! A number of national champions have represented small geographical areas.

History of the National Spelling Bee

The National Spelling Bee began in 1925 with nine contestants. It was sponsored by the Louisville *Courier-Journal,* which had conducted a statewide match to find the best grade-school spellers in Kentucky, and then decided to extend a challenge to other newspapers to choose their own champions to take part in a spelling showdown in Washington, D.C., to determine a national champion. The *Detroit News,* the *Akron Beacon Journal,* the *South Bend News-Times,* and the *Hartford Times* were also among the sponsors that first year.

In 1941, Scripps Newspapers took over sponsorship of the National Spelling Bee. There was no Scripps National Spelling Bee during the war years of 1943–45.

The first national champion was eleven-year-old Frank Neuhauser of Louisville, Kentucky, who in 1925 correctly spelled *gladiolus* to beat out eight other contestants and win $500 in $20 gold pieces. As national champion, he shook hands with President Calvin Coolidge. He went

Food and Cooking

LEVEL: Beginning

applesauce
aspic
burrito
caramelize
casserole
cheesesteak
clambake
condiment
cornflakes
dinette
dumpling
gourmet
homogenize
kickshaw
luncheon
macrobiotics
marmalade
pandowdy
percolator
piquant
pumpernickel
ravioli
refreshments
scampi
shortening
subgum
sundae
sushi
tapioca
tortilla
venison
vinegar

A number of national champions have represented small geographical areas.

P-H-O-O-E-Y!

Each of the words below was misspelled at the end of a National Spelling Bee, making the difference between first and second place.

apotropaic
cervicorn
chrysanthemum
cortile
crescive
dyscalculia
farrago
geophagy
glitch
morigeration
oligarchy
onomastics
opsimath
parvenuism
philippic
prairillon
ratatouille
resipiscence
Roscian
schwarmerei
senescing
seriatim
sesquipedalian
trouvaille
velleity
virescence

on to study electrical engineering, and later he became a patent attorney. Mr. Neuhauser, who turned 92 in 2006, says that since his triumph he has always grown gladiolus in his garden.

Hey, Maybe I Could Win!

Whether you're talking about your school bee, a local bee, or the National Spelling Bee finals in Washington, D.C., one thing's for sure—the person who *will* win one day is thinking the same thing right now: "It could be me!" But becoming a spelling champion doesn't mean spending a couple of afternoons with a computer game. It's a major project.

Scratch any spelling bee contestant and you'll find a regular kid, a cool kid—one who loves basketball, plays the trumpet, likes Mexican food, has a Labrador puppy, or dresses as Voldemort or Buffy the Vampire Slayer for Halloween. What do spelling bee winners do that's different from most kids? They read for fun— a lot—and they care about getting words right. Are you up for that?

As you go through this book, you'll likely see many new words. If some of them seem difficult, you're in good company, so don't be intimidated. You can learn them just as you learned the multiplication tables: by memorizing them. But just as math facts are interrelated, so are words, and the more you know about how they're related, the better you'll remember how to spell them. We'll show you how to get more information about the words you study.

If you're ready to become a word whiz, let's get started! First, a few tips: In this book, we sometimes use the term **phoneme,** meaning "the smallest unit of speech that distinguishes one utterance from another," when we discuss the various spellings of a sound. For example, the phoneme /f/ is usually spelled *f* or *ph* at the beginning of a word; but it can sometimes be spelled *gh,* as in *laugh,* at the end of a word. To indicate the **spelling** of example words, we use italic letters: *cat.* To show a **pronunciation** using phonemes, we use forward slashes: /kat/. (The linguist's term for that slash, by the way, is *virgule*—a word whose Latin root means "small rod.") Occasionally, we use quotes to designate

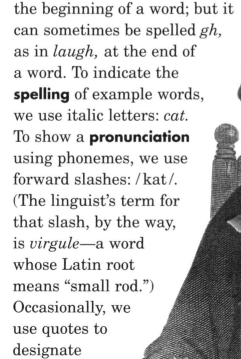

So What's It Like to Be a Champion?

"**B**eing a spelling champion is a wonderful thing. It gives you two pillars of identity that will last you your whole life. First, you are a speller, a conscientious person who cares about the details, an authority that other people count on and turn to.

"*Fee fi phoneme. Words aren't always spelled like they seem.*"

Second, you are a champion, a hard worker, an ambitious performer who saw a thing through to the end and won the rewards, at whatever level."

—HENRY FELDMAN, *1960 National Spelling Bee champion* (winning word: **eudaemonic**)

A Close Call

"I want to tell younger students that they should never give up. The spelling bee has a huge luck factor, and it's very likely that you'll be asked to spell words that you don't know. It's hard work to study for another year, but it's certainly worth it."

KERRY CLOSE,
2006 National Spelling Bee champion
(winning word: **Ursprache**)

some sounds, such as "uh" for the **schwa,** for which linguists would use a special symbol, or symbols, instead of English letters. If this sounds confusing now, it should all become clear somewhere around Chapter 3.

Good luck!

CHAPTER 2

Becoming a Champion

*An investment in knowledge
pays the best interest.*
—BENJAMIN FRANKLIN

"Okay, everybody, tomorrow is our classroom spelling bee and the winner will represent us in the school spelling bee next week."

The road that leads to the National Spelling Bee usually starts here, in a classroom bee. If you're reading this book, chances are you've already participated in one.

Master Little Things, Get Bigger Things Right

"Spelling is terribly important. It is the essence of sincere attention to whatever you are doing. It gives you confidence and gratification to do a simple thing well and know that you got the right outcome. If you master the little things, then you may be able to get the bigger things right, and at the very least you will know that you got the details right repeatedly."

—HENRY FELDMAN, *1960 National Spelling Bee champion*

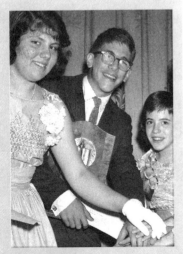

Henry, 1960.

If you like to read and have already done well on spelling quizzes, you're an excellent candidate for spelling bee success. This chapter is all about increasing your chances of it!

There are two basic strategies for doing well in any spelling bee. First, **be prepared.** Find out exactly when and where your spelling bee will take place and put it on your calendar. Second, **set up your study area and get to work.** Even if your classroom bee is tomorrow, you can still put in some vocabulary study time and improve your chance of winning. Your teacher may decide to use spelling words you've had during the year, so look over your spelling tests and quizzes if you've saved them. Note the words you missed, and make sure you know them cold.

If you can, get a copy of the Scripps National Spelling Bee booklet *Spell It!* Your teacher or your school's spelling bee coordinator should be able to help you, or check the Scripps National Spelling Bee Web site, www.spellingbee.com. The words in this study booklet have been chosen specifically for the classroom and school level, so you will already know many of them. This makes it a great tool for practicing spelling aloud. See if you can get your parents, a sibling, or a friend to read the words for you to spell (bribe them, if you have to—chocolate works well). Maybe you and a friend or two can even set up and act out a mock spelling bee with real words, as you take turns being the pronouncer and making up sentences.

If you're preparing for a school spelling bee and you're already familiar with the words in *Spell It!*, keep studying! Start by carefully reading Chapter 5 in this book. When you look at the examples, try to think of some that aren't already represented. For instance, the rule may be, "Drop the final silent *e* of a word when adding a suffix that begins with a vowel, but keep the *e* if the suffix begins with a consonant." If the example given in the book is *advise / advising / advisement,* come up with a few others such as *leave / leaving / leaves* and *false / falsify / falsehood.*

❝Keep the e *when the suffix begins with a consonant!*❞

The Four Types of Tricky Words

The words that most people misspell generally fall into four categories: exceptions to well-known spelling rules, like **seize;** words with double letters, like **accommodate;** words with silent letters, like **subpoena;** and words containing a schwa (the usually unstressed vowel sound "uh"), like **separate** ("SEP-uh-ruht"). Outside those main categories, a few words, like **fiery,** change the root spelling when a suffix is added; and some words, like **hypocrisy,** are just plain hard!

You don't want to *memorize* the rules—you want them to become second nature so that you never have to think about them consciously.

How the Octothorp Got Its "e"

In 2002, *Webster's Third New International Dictionary* was updated. The only changes—the first since 1993—were in the addenda section, where most of the changes had to do with the addition of new words.

Octothorp, the name for the symbol that is commonly known as the pound sign (check out the bottom right button on your telephone), was updated with a variant spelling. In the 1993 version of the addenda section, the only listing was *octothorp*. Now two spellings are listed: *octothorp* and *octothorpe*.

Admittedly, this part may seem a little dull, but examples reinforce concepts. So come up with the snappiest, most memorable examples you can. If there are particular rules you have a hard time remembering how to apply, you can set yourself the task of writing a silly poem to illustrate a rule:

The funniest boys have said,
"Unless you've been dropped on your head,
A single vowel *y*
Means change it to *i*
Before *-est, -ness, -hood, -ly,* or *-ed.*"

This particular ditty will never win any limerick prizes, but it contains the essential information: the rule  (when *y* is the lone vowel at the end of a word, it is changed to *i* before most suffixes); an example *(funny/funniest);* and an opposite example *(boy/boys,* where the *y* is not the only vowel at the end and so remains unchanged).

Of course, the work you do to come up with examples helps consolidate them in your mind. You don't want to *memorize* the rules—*way* too boring! You want them to become second nature so that you never have to think about them consciously. If you're already a good speller who has internalized many spelling rules, stretch yourself by finding exceptions to each rule. This is a good way to start studying some of the—drum roll, please—Weird Words in English,

starting of course with the word *weird,* which is an exception to the rule "*i* before *e,* except after *c* or when sounded like *a.*"

Next, read the front section of a city newspaper. Don't just skim it; pay close attention to the words used and to their spellings. Teachers like to keep education relevant to the larger world, so your school bee is very unlikely to be harder than the level of the average newspaper.

1958 *Winner Jolitta Schlehuber of Topeka, Kansas, (winning word:* **syllepsis**) *receives her check.*

Weird Words

It gets a lot weirder than the rule-breaker word *weird*. What could be odder than a word that seemingly comes from nowhere? The words below have no known origin. Some of them are familiar and some are spelled the way they sound, but others leave you stranded without even a root word to hang on to.

askarel
balderdash
bamboozle
bumicky
curmudgeon
flabbergast
gremlin
gyascutus
hobbledehoy
huckaback
humbug
jitney
kentledge
lobscouse
marrowsky
mumblebee
murre
quandary
scrivello
shenanigan
shrivel
tantivy
wingding
yegg

Hand the newspaper to a friend or parent and ask this person to give you a short spelling quiz from it. Your questioner can select twenty or so words for you to spell aloud. If you haven't done this kind of spelling practice before, welcome to the world of *How to Spell Like a Champ.* Most spelling bee contestants spend part of their study time spelling aloud with another person giving them the words. It's one of the most effective ways to practice, because it gives you a feel for spelling aloud and doesn't allow you to fool yourself about knowing the words. If you can, do this for a few minutes each day before

1992 *Amanda Goad, 13, holds up her trophy after correctly spelling* **lyceum.**

Try to have a strong mental picture of yourself correctly spelling each word aloud onstage.

the classroom bee. If words from the newspaper are easy for you, you're well on your way. If they're not, you just need to practice, practice, practice! Here's another thing you need to do: Practice!

You should also find a good list of commonly misspelled words (like the handy one in Chapter 5) and try to learn them all. *Doing this may be the smartest move of your entire spelling career.* Many a school spelling bee has hinged on an everyday word like *occurence, embarass,* or *athalete.* These words are in some ways harder to learn and remember than long, seemingly super-tough words—but they're used frequently, so get them right. (Hope you noticed that *occurrence, embarrass,* and *athlete* were misspelled. Just checking to see if you're paying attention!) Years from now, when you're in high school and are looking for jobs and applying to colleges, you'll be glad you studied commonly misspelled words, because misspelling a simple word can be very embarrassing. (People who use computers often spell-check their documents, but not that many spell-check their outgoing e-mail or thank-you notes to college admissions officers!) Ask your parents, teachers, and friends which words have been the hardest for them to learn to spell correctly, and learn those, too.

As you work through all of these steps, always keep a running list of the words you've

Here are nineteen school- or local-level spelling words, taken from the front page of *The New York Times* on an average day. Don't peek—just hand the book to someone who will read the words for you to spell. How did you do?

adamantly
anonymity
catalytic
chaos
consolidate
cudgel
diaspora
dominance
evacuee
incumbent
memorandum
mosaic
ostensibly
polygraph
scenario
submission
subsidiary
tirade
transgressions

Bee Seasons

SCHOOL BEES:
January–February

LOCAL AND REGIONAL BEES:
March

THE SCRIPPS NATIONAL
SPELLING BEE: **late May or
early June**

had the most trouble learning. If you write them down and look at them often enough, you'll find they become the easiest words to remember.

Another strategy for doing well in spelling bees is to *chill*. Just relax. Follow a routine that makes you feel calm. Get a little exercise the day before the bee—play tennis or soccer, ride your bike, take a walk, whatever. Have a nice dinner, then do something fun. It's fine to have one last short study session before bed, but don't stay up late. As you study, try to have a strong mental picture of yourself correctly spelling each word aloud onstage in your school auditorium or wherever the spelling bee is being held. Then set the alarm to get you up with enough time to get ready for school without being rushed.

On the morning of the spelling bee, eat a good breakfast that includes some protein so that your blood sugar doesn't take a big dive after you get to school. If you want to look over your list of tricky words, spend just a little time with it before you leave home. You don't want to drag your list around with you and read it at the last minute before the bee starts; that will just make you feel desperate, not well prepared.

It's a good idea to go to the restroom well before the spelling bee begins so that you don't get rushed and distracted at the last minute. Look at yourself in the restroom mirror and see yourself as a champion! A positive attitude may not ensure spelling bee success, but it beats the effect that a pessimistic attitude can have.

If you've taken the above steps to study for your classroom or school bee, you can feel confident in your preparation. If you are nervous, stretch a little and take some deep breaths before spelling begins. Each time you sail through a word, try to enjoy the process as much as you can. The words may get harder as you go along, but competing will get easier.

Moving Up the Ladder

If you win your school bee, you will be moving on to a city, county, or regional bee—perhaps all three. Usually, you will have at least a week, perhaps several, between your school bee and the next bee. Put all the details of the next bee—date, time, and place—on your calendar, and get your study tools in order. If you haven't started a spelling notebook yet, this is a good time to do it! See "Organizing a Spelling Notebook" in Chapter 3 for details on organizing and using it.

Decide now how much time you would like to spend preparing for your spelling bee participation.

A Sort of Mental Scoreboard

"My main way of learning words was just to read as much as I could. I used to read a lot of books from English publishers, and I picked up some relatively obscure words from that. I used to read a lot of history books, too; still do, for that matter. One of the words I got in the national bee was **hussar**, which I had seen in one of the books I got from England. Another word I got in the contest was **chinook**, which I remembered from the salmon-egg bait we used to buy when we went trout fishing in Colorado. I had a mental trick that I used pretty effectively in the contest: Before I tried to spell a word I would visualize it appearing a letter at a time on a sort of mental scoreboard. That helped me avoid hasty mistakes."

—ROBIN KRAL,
1972 National Spelling Bee champion
(winning word: **macerate**)

The Note Card Solution

"My mom prepared note cards for me to review whenever I had a spare moment. I also remember keeping note cards tucked in whatever books I was reading so that I could write down 'good words,' and I still do this!"

—PEG MCCARTHY,
1978 National Spelling Bee champion
(winning word: **deification**)

Peg, 1978.

You're representing your school now, not just yourself, so if you don't try, you might disappoint others—especially your teachers, who are probably quite proud of you, as well as the student who would be representing your school if you hadn't participated in the first place. You don't want to have any regrets later about your performance, so determine how much time per day, or over the period of a week, is reasonable for you to dedicate to spelling. You can adjust this goal as your studying progresses. After a week or two, you will know whether you wish to increase or decrease your time. Try your best to stick to your goal until you decide that a different plan will suit you better.

It may seem as though you're giving up a lot for spelling, especially if you have to suspend other activities and turn down party invitations to study, but remember, it's only temporary (and some of those parties probably turned out

to be lame, anyway). School bees typically begin in January; local and regional bees must be completed by the beginning of April. In late May or early June a national champion is crowned.

Can You Spell *arcuate fasciculus*?

Have you ever been called a "brain" by your friends? If you're a good speller, a better nickname might be "Broca" or "Wernicke." They're the two areas of the brain responsible for language functions, including spelling. Complex brain functions like spelling don't arise in a "center" or single area in the brain; rather, circuits connecting multiple areas of the brain are responsible for most complex behaviors.

When the pronouncer gives a word, the sound waves enter your ears and strike the tympanum (also known as the eardrum). This causes the three small bones of the inner ear to vibrate and pass the vibrations to the cochlea, where the vibrations are converted to bioelectric signals, or nerve impulses, inside the organ of Corti. The impulses travel through the eighth cranial nerve to the primary auditory cortex, then to Wernicke's area, where the word's phonemes and syllabic stresses are recognized. (Wernicke's area also processes written language—but in that case, the information comes from the optic nerve and the primary visual cortex.)

The information then travels along a pathway of nerve fibers, known as the arcuate fasciculus, to Broca's area, which interprets the information and formulates a response. Broca's area transmits a signal to the primary motor cortex, which controls the voluntary muscles, to produce speech (in an oral spelling bee) or writing (in a written bee).

To get the best performance out of your brain during a spelling bee, you need to start well ahead of time with a good diet and plenty of sleep and exercise. On competition day, eat a breakfast with complex carbohydrates (think fruit, oatmeal, or whole grain cereal), which have been shown to aid memory; and protein, which will help keep your blood sugar steady. Once the spelling bee is under way, drink water during the breaks, because your brain needs it to conduct electrical signals. If you get tired, stretch in your seat and take some deep breaths— oxygen is brain food.

When Do I Eat and Sleep?

There's no question about it: The more study time you put in, the more you will learn, and the better you will do in spelling competition. However, there are definitely trade-offs! If you're studying hard, keeping a spelling notebook, and practicing spelling aloud, sometimes it may seem as though spelling has taken over your life. It's not easy to balance school, extracurricular activities, and practicing for any kind of big contest.

If you have athletics, music lessons, or other activities in addition to classes and homework, you may not have much time to sit down and study words for an uninterrupted period on a daily basis. If so, you'll need to find creative ways to fit numerous small bursts of spelling study into your schedule. Here are a few ideas:

- Have brief daily study sessions during the week, and a longer one (or two) on weekends.

- Keep a study list in your pocket or backpack that you can pull out and go over when you're waiting somewhere. Make sure you update this list frequently, so that you're not studying the same words over and over.

Most spelling bee contestants spend part of their study time spelling aloud with another person giving them the words.

- Ask friends and neighbors to try a new word on you every time they see you and to keep track of the ones you miss so that they can ask you again. This is good practice for spelling words that come out of the blue!

- Ask teachers if you may study your word list quietly when you've finished your class work. They may be willing to let you, especially if you ask them to give you a list of good spelling words that pertain to their subject.

- Tape a short list of practice words to the bathroom mirror and go over it while you're brushing your teeth. Change this list every day. You might want to use this brief time to study a group of words that share a common root or affix or that have the same language of origin.

- If you have a computer, see if you can find a screensaver that will let you enter words that will scroll across your screen when your computer is idle. Enter a new set of "problem" words every couple of days. The more you see the correct spelling of these words, even when you aren't consciously thinking about them, the more they will become fixed in your memory.

"This One Trivial Thing"

"My dad gave me some advice I will never forget. He first explained to me how proud he was of my achievements already. Then he said, 'You have to realize, Wendy, how much *chance* plays in the bee. You may know every other word in your round, but if you don't know the next one on the word list, you will be doomed. You are no less of a person, or a speller for that matter, for not knowing that one word. You have to think beyond this one trivial thing. What you have *learned* is most important. *That* is the ultimate measurement of whether you have truly won.'"

—WENDY GUEY,
1996 National Spelling Bee champion
(winning word: **vivisepulture**)

Guess what? Your parents have been telling the truth all along. It turns out it really *is* important to eat well and get enough sleep. British studies have shown that teenagers who eat sugary foods in the morning perform like an average seventy-year-old on tests of memory and attention. Using the spelling bee as an excuse to grab dough-nuts instead of eating a real breakfast will backfire! And scientists at Harvard University and elsewhere have made a very interesting discovery: A good night's

sleep on the night after you've learned some-thing new will help you store that information in long-term memory; otherwise, the material may simply pass out of the brain. For your studying to pay off, you need to hit the hay on time every night. Making up for lost sleep on subsequent nights doesn't work, so don't try to pull all-nighters, even occasionally. Good habits are worth the time you put into them. It's hard enough winning spelling bees *without* having the brain of a seventy-year-old.

CHAPTER 3

Becoming More Serious

If you're just looking for tips on winning a school bee, and even thinking about the National Spelling Bee makes you nervous—skip this section! Do not under any circumstances read this! Are you reading this? No? Good. We wouldn't want to scare you off. But we have some great study tips for kids who are shooting for the stars.

Music

LEVEL: Beginning

acoustic
bolero
cadence
chopsticks
choral
chord
coda
contralto
descant
Dixieland
gutbucket
hula
hymnal
instrumental
keyboard
marimba
metronome
monotonic
octave
organology
reggae
resonant
sonata
songwriter
subinterval
symphonic
tempered
tenor
tonality
treble
vibraphone
viola
woodshed
woodwind

NOW APPEARING
COUNTRY'S BEST SPELLER

Once upon a time, excellent spellers stood a reasonably good chance of making it to the national finals in their first year of competition. Well, that was then and this is now. Spelling itself may not have changed in the last few decades, but many other things have. Bigger prizes, more publicity, and a bit of Hollywood glamour have conspired to make spelling a very hot academic activity right now. There's tougher competition than ever before, so if you want to go to the National Spelling Bee, you need to start preparing as early as possible. It's increasingly common not only for national finalists to have competed in the national bee more than once (though a few newspaper sponsors have an eligibility rule limiting a speller to one trip to the nationals), but also for them to have competed at the local level for two years or more before they won a regional bee. You need to set goals that are both ambitious and realistic to keep progressing happily in your spelling career.

Dictionaries

Let's get one thing straight: You're not getting to the finals without a dictionary. It's the one study tool you absolutely must

Words in the addenda section of *Webster's Third* are frequently found on National Spelling Bee word lists. A word to the wise is sufficient.

have to advance beyond your school bee. You can find great study words in many places, but if you cannot look them up, you will learn nothing except how to spell them. The more you *know* about the words you study, the better you will remember them. If you don't have access to a dictionary at home, you may want to do your word study at the library.

If you are very serious about spelling bee competition, you may want to buy a new dictionary. In any case, you should know that the Scripps National Spelling Bee uses the most recent edition of *Webster's Third New International Dictionary of the English Language, Unabridged,* and its addenda section as the authority for the spelling of words. **Words not listed in this dictionary and its addenda will not appear on any word list used in Scripps National Spelling**

ords in the addenda section of *Webster's Third* are frequently found on National Spelling Bee word lists. A word to the wise is sufficient.

"It's my Third New International Dictionary, Unabridged, *or nothing.***"**

Waiting for Webster's Fourth

Webster's Third New International Dictionary is a descriptive dictionary. Spellings listed in *Webster's Third* describe what is most often seen in print as a correct spelling. When the editors of *Webster's Third* updated the addenda section, they had seen enough examples of **octothorpe** in print to decide that the spelling of this word was just as acceptable as **octothorp.** Thus a variant spelling was added.

Bottom line: Be sure you're using the most recent version of *Webster's Third New International Dictionary* as you prepare.

Note of interest: The editors at Merriam-Webster are currently working on *Webster's Fourth New International Dictionary.* Changes will not be limited to the addenda section. When this dictionary becomes available (no date has been set), it will be the official dictionary of the Scripps National Spelling Bee.

Bee competition. You can certainly use another dictionary to study, because there is a great deal of overlap between dictionaries; but there will be some words in other dictionaries that are either not in *Webster's Third* or are listed with alternate spellings. Similarly, there are words in *Webster's Third* that do not appear in other dictionaries, particularly abridged dictionaries. Therefore, there will almost certainly be gaps in your preparation for advanced spelling bee competition if you do not have access to *Webster's Third.*

An excellent option for computer users is *Webster's Third* on CD-ROM. Using an electronic dictionary for your word study has some outstanding advantages. You can search the *Webster's Third* CD-ROM according to any of thirteen different criteria, either alone or in combination. For example, you can find words that entered English from Portuguese or narrow your search down to just adjectives that entered English from Portuguese. This will help you understand Portuguese spelling patterns. Another possibility is to find all words that contain a particular root or suffix. This flexibility has a huge impact on the way you study. When you find a word you don't know, it's easy to look up words that are related to it. When you see words presented in related groups, it's much easier to remember their meanings and spellings.

All national finalists receive a copy of *Webster's Third* before the finals in Washington, D.C., but if becoming a national finalist is your goal, start using this dictionary much earlier. By the time you become a national finalist and win a copy, the finals will be just around the corner. If you become the happy owner of a duplicate copy, you can always donate it to a friend, another speller, or your school library—or just keep an extra dic-

Applauding the winners at a statewide Illinois "fingerspelling bee" for deaf students.

tionary in the den or kitchen of your home. You never know where you'll be when the urge to look up a word strikes.

Read, read, read. Any magazine, book, or newspaper you pick up may contain your next spelling bee word.

Copies of *Webster's Third,* in hardcover and on CD-ROM, can usually be found at online bookstores or large chain bookstores for a discounted price. The Scripps National Spelling Bee will always take its words from the most recent edition, so check to be sure that the one you're getting is the "latest and greatest."

Other Useful Tools

If you have a computer and use e-mail, get your parents' permission to sign up for a few free "word of the day" services. There are a number of good ones. You can subscribe to Merriam-Webster's Word of the Day at www.m-w.com. (In fact, you'll want to look this site over care-

1926 *President Coolidge welcomes a group of school children who took part in the second National Spelling Bee. The winner was Pauline Bell of Louisville, Kentucky, who correctly spelled the word* **abrogate,** *winning two gold medals and $1,000.*

fully; it also has free crosswords and other vocabulary-building games. Merriam-Webster has a language arts site for students at www.wordcentral.com.) These services can be great vocabulary builders because they almost always offer some memorable pieces of information about the words.

Check with your school's spelling bee coordinator, who may have other materials that could help you, such as notes or word lists from previous local or regional bees. And remember: What goes around comes around. As you progress in spelling, it's a nice gesture to give a copy of any word lists you collect to the coordinator. The next student to represent your school in spelling bees will be very grateful.

Finally, the best thing you can do to hone your spelling is to read, read, read. Every magazine, book, or newspaper you pick up may contain your next spelling bee word.

Organizing a Spelling Notebook

What kind of organizer are you? Do you enjoy putting together binders with colored divider tabs, colored paper, and colored labels down the spine? Or do you prefer creating and labeling nested folders on your computer and making a shortcut to them on

Ibuprofen and Sousaphones

"Studying is important, but sometimes paying attention to the words in the world around you can help you just as much. For example, I knew how to spell **sousaphone** because I was in band and I knew about the instrument's connection to John Philip Sousa. I knew how to spell **ibuprofen** because I paid attention to commercials for cold medicine. I knew how to spell **kaolinic** because I had heard about how kaolin was used to make clay pipes when my parents took me on a trip to Busch Gardens and Colonial Williamsburg."

—JON PENNINGTON,
1986 National Spelling Bee champion
(winning word: **odontalgia**)

Bee Lucky

"I'd advise kids who want to win to study all they can, to learn root words and word origins, and to practice guessing at words they don't know. I'd also advise them to be happy with however the results come out—there is an element of luck in winning spelling bees!"

—STEPHANIE PETIT,
1987 National Spelling Bee champion
(winning word:
staphylococci*)*

the computer desktop? Think hard about what comes naturally to you. If you're going to study seriously for a spelling bee, you may want to put together a spelling notebook—either a physical or a virtual one—and your system should reflect the way *you* learn best.

If you are a visual learner, you'll generally remember words you've seen once. (If you're very visual, you may have a photographic memory. You may even remember what page a word was on in a book you've read or where the word fell on the page!) In fact, you might find that all you need to study effectively is as many word lists as you can get and a partner to quiz you on them. Still, no one's perfect, and you'll want to keep track of any words you have trouble with so that you can review them a couple of times. The act of typing them into a file or writing them in a spiral-bound notebook once or a few times may be all you need to fix them in your memory.

Most people, however, don't have photographic memories, and a carefully planned notebook system can help them learn words much more efficiently than going over and over lists of words at random. Remember: The faster you

Organization is a process, not a single act.

can learn words, the more words you can learn.

Don't worry if at first it seems like you're spending a lot of time organizing. As you study, the plan that suits you best will unfold. Organization is a process, not a single act. The advantage of setting up this kind of coordinated study is that having done it once for spelling, you'll know what works for you, and you'll be able to do it in the future for any other subject you decide you want to master.

There's an art to note-taking for your spelling notebook. When you take notes for school subjects, you probably start at the top of the page and keep taking notes until the class is over. The next time you take notes in that class, you probably just start where you left off and write some more. But you will learn more from your spelling note-taking if you designate areas in which to put different types of infor-mation, so that you can look them up easily later. If you like binders for organizing, use one that allows you to move pages and add paper. (You'll appreciate this flexibility if you decide halfway through your studying to change your organization scheme.) To start out, you might like to have one large binder and use dividers for each category of information. As your

Letter Perfect

Did you ever realize that the consonants of the alphabet have names that can be spelled?

bee
cee
dee
ef
gee
aitch
jay
kay (also ka)
el
em
en
pee
cue
ar
ess (or es)
tee
vee
double-u (or double-you)
ex
wye (or wy)
zee

spelling notebook grows, you might move it to several smaller binders, one for each category or group of categories.

If you have access to a computer at home and do most of your studying when a keyboard is within reach, you can take notes electronically. Assign a folder on the computer for each category or chapter of your notebook. When the occasion to take a note arises, you can click on the chapter to which you would like to add information. Or, if necessary, you can quickly create a new chapter for the note at hand. This electronic note-taking method saves space and might save time. It also allows for fast searching and instant alphabetization of words within a chapter.

Mathew L. Roca, below right, lines up with 79 other New York City elementary school spelling bee contestants, in the final round of the 41st Annual **Daily News** *New York Citywide Spelling Bee.*

The point is not necessarily to enter every word you study into the notebook. Rather, it's to record words that interest you, either because you find them difficult or because something about them strikes you as an interesting pattern. Initially, you will probably make lists of individual words that give you problems. As you begin to learn more about the composition of words, you may want to make lists of spelling rules and exceptions, root words and their derivatives, words that came to English from particular languages, and so forth. You can probably come up with more categories of your own. (Throw in some fun ones—"NBA Words," "Words from TV," "Palindromes," or words from your favorite series of books.) And you may want to add the same words to multiple categories—for example, *vinaigrette* might go into three categories: "French Words," "Food Words," and "Words Ending in *-et / -ette.*"

When you are reading books, magazines, and newspapers for pleasure, you will frequently run across new words that fit into one of your categories or perhaps give you an idea for a new category for your notebook system. Carry a little notebook with you or keep some scratch

adagio
allargando
allemande
animato
arabesque
Brahmsian
brillante
cadenza
clavier
coloratura
conjunto
doloroso
duple
flamenco
Handelian
libretto
ligature
mariachi
melomania
musicale
pastiche
polska
preludio
psalmist
reprise
schmaltz
sinistra
skirl
staccato
strophic
syncopate
tardo
tremolo
xylophone

Finding Your Rhythm

"I tried a lot of different spelling speeds the first couple of years I competed—spelling slowly, spelling fast, spelling three letters at a time. I finally realized that when spelling aloud, I mentally 'see' the word on a blank page; it's as though I'm just reading off the letters. Once I knew that, I was able to settle into a natural rhythm when spelling. It's important to find your own rhythm and practice it consciously when you study, to help you retain the word. If you spell a word in competition with the same rhythm you use to successfully spell it in a practice session, it's hard to go wrong."

—Barrie Trinkle, *1973 National Spelling Bee champion* (winning word: **vouchsafe**)

paper handy [if you're not one of those kids who has a personal digital assistant (PDA) on hand at all times]; you can transfer the words to your notebook or computer later. You can use a cell phone or cell-phone camera to quickly store the spelling of an interesting word to add to your computer notebook later. You can also buy a miniature recorder just for this purpose at very low cost.

Here's a set of examples—one possible organization for your study notebook. Many of these grouping and category suggestions came from recent spelling bee contestants, but you'll certainly come up with more categories on your own, based on your personal interests and what kinds of words you find challenging.

Suffixes

words ending in *-ar/-er/-or*
words ending in *-ary/-ery/-ory*
words ending in *-ance/-ence* and *-ant/-ent*
words ending in *-yze/-ize/-ise*
words ending in *-gue/-g*
words ending in *-ean/-ian*
words ending in *-ese/-ise*
words ending in *-eous/-ious*
words ending in *-able/-ible*

words beginning with *dis-/dys-*
words beginning with *pari-/peri-*

words from African languages *(tsetse, safari)*
words from French *(armoire, avalanche, bombardier)*
words with French suffixes *(-ure, -eur, -oir, -aise, -erie, -et/-ette)*
words from Japanese *(pachinko, tatami, sayonara)*
words from Portuguese *(sargasso, ipecac, mandarin)*
words from Spanish *(simpatico, hacienda, matador)*

Four spellers from New York congratulate winner Robin Kral of Lubbock, Texas, at the 45th Annual National Spelling Bee. From left are Alison Baldwin of Westchester County, Eric Sohn of Long Island, Robin, Maria DiGiovanni of New York, and Vincent Vaiano of New York.

It Takes Two

"I recommend avoiding the rut of memorizing word lists and asking someone to test you on the words you've memorized. Instead, play spelling bee every day. Ask someone to give you words of *their* choosing, words that you possibly haven't studied. In spelling bees you have to spell words of the officials' choosing, not your own, so why not practice for that experience on a regular basis? Stick with the method and in time you will develop confidence. That will make you a better thinker for those uncomfortable moments in competition when you're asked to spell an unfamiliar word."

—PAIGE PIPKIN KIMBLE, *1981 National Spelling Bee champion and current Scripps National Spelling Bee director* (winning word: **sarcophagus**)

Other origins

words of unknown origin *(bamboozle, bungee, quandary)*

words with an imitative origin *(froufrou, hooroosh, kyoodle, whippoorwill)*

Meaning

words from classical mythology and history *(auroral, hector, iridescent, pegasus)*

words for different breeds of dogs *(weimaraner, schnauzer, Chihuahua)*

words about games and sports *(badminton, croquet, kibitzer, mancala, pinochle)*

food words [try organizing these under various subcategories, such as vegetables *(cassava, rutabaga, asparagus)*; cheeses *(Gorgonzola, provolone, Wensleydale)*; pasta shapes *(capellini, fusilli, tagliatelle)*; beverages *(orangeade, mocha, sarsaparilla)*; desserts *(ambrosia, pandowdy, cannoli)*]

G-O-R-G-O-N

music words *(pizzicato, schottische, mariachi)*

words for flowers and plants *(geranium, epiphyte, bromeliad)*

words for dinosaurs *(ankylosaur, diplodocus, deinonychus)*

scientific words *(aerolithology, hydraulics, rhinolaryngology)*

words for occupations and careers *(magistrate, phlebotomist, amanuensis)*

geographical terms *(orography, guyot, estuary)*

names of diseases *(malaria, diphtheria, trichinosis)*

anatomy words *(viscera, pituitary, eustachian)*

Bee nice.

Life Lessons

"In the months following my win, I learned many 'life skills': how to conduct myself in the public eye, how to interact with the media, and how to take compliment after compliment. But as much as I learned in those months, I learned even more from my two trips to the Comfort Room. Life is not holding the trophy aloft for a fleeting moment. Life is the Comfort Room and what surrounds it. You give it your best shot, you pause briefly to gather your strength, and you come back and try to do better than you did the time before. And no matter how well you do, there will always be someone better than you."

—NED ANDREWS,
1994 National Spelling Bee champion
(winning word: antediluvian)

commonly confused homonyms *(stationary / stationery, complement / compliment)*

words with silent first letters *(ptarmigan, mnemonic, gnathic, knickerbocker)*

words that are often mispronounced *(mischievous, nuclear, pronunciation)*

capitalized words *(Armageddon, Britishism, Rubicon)*

interesting words from Shakespeare *(dastard, argosy, demesne)*

portmanteau words *(avionics, biodiversity, stagflation)*

eponyms *(begonia, nicotine, poinsettia)*

words that are illustrated in *Webster's Third*

words with double *i* *(foliiform, incurvariid, biischial)*

words with *oe* and *ae* combinations *(Croesus, chaeta)*

words with double *u* *(vacuum, continuum, duumvirate)*

exceptions to the "*i* before *e*" rule *(Anaheim, foreign, height, seismic, weird)*

verbs that end in *c* and add a *k* before *-ing* and *-ed* *(picnic, panic, bivouac)*

words with troublesome double letters *(aardvark, millennium)*

Turn off the iPod and the phone, and disable Instant Messaging.

nouns that end in a vowel and *k (anorak, batik)* or a vowel and *c (ipecac, havoc)*
words whose root spelling changes when you add an affix *(pollen / pollinate)*
short but difficult words of three, four, and five letters *(aitch, mho, bloc)*

The $64,000 Interrogatory

ow long do serious spellers study every day? That's the $64,000 question. Well, it varies greatly. To study for a school bee, a speller might look over word lists for fifteen or twenty minutes per night for a week. Spellers who really want to win their local or regional bee often study at least an hour or two per day as their qualifying bees approach. Even more serious spellers who are heading for the National Spelling Bee may spend a month or more studying as much as four to six hours per day. Some feel they will learn the most if they

Mail Order Words

f you know someone who is on mailing lists for catalogs, ask if you can have the catalogs after they've been read. Catalogs can be a gold mine of good spelling bee words.

Take **Limoges,** a 1998 National Spelling Bee word that appeared near the very end of the competition. Miniature hinged Limoges boxes made of porcelain, and relatively inexpensive takeoffs on the genuine, appear in many catalogs.

Item descriptions in catalogs can provide you many new words to study. Grab a stack of catalogs and start making a list of all the words you think would be good spelling bee words. Before you add them to your spelling notebook, though, look up each word in *Webster's Third.* Make sure that there is an entry for the word and that the word and its spelling meet the criteria listed in the National Spelling Bee rules.

Portmanteau Math: Chuckle + Snort = Chortle

Portmanteau Words

Portmanteau is a fancy word for *suitcase.* It was originally French, and came from two words that meant "to carry" and "mantle" (a mantle is a large cloak)—much like *suitcase,* which is a case for a suit! The phrase *portmanteau word* means "a word composed of [1] parts of two words (as *chortle* from *chuckle* and *snort*), [2] all of one word and part of another (as *bookmobile* from *book* and *automobile*), or [3] two entire words, and characterized—invariably in the latter case and frequently in the two former cases—by single occurrence of one or more sounds or letters that appear in both the component words (as *motel* from *motor hotel,* *camporee* from *camp* and *jamboree, aniseed* from *anise seed*)." Have you noticed an interesting fact about *portmanteau*? It and its synonym *suitcase* are both portmanteau words!

spread their studying throughout the year; others like to start just before the school bee and work intensely for a few months.

However you decide to study spelling, you will learn better if you follow some common-sense study policies. First, do your formal studying in a quiet place where you won't be distracted. Turn off the iPod and the phone, and disable Instant Messaging (IM). Listening to music and trying to ignore IMs while you're concentrating on words is too much multitasking for your Broca's and Wernicke's areas.

You may want to break your studying into short sessions and do two of them per day. Or, if you have a number of brief times during the day when you look at a list of words—say at the breakfast table or on the bus—you may find it's enough to have just one formal sit-down study session per day. You should have at least one, though, so that you can take stock of what you've done and what you need to study next. It's hard to do that on the fly.

And don't forget to give yourself occasional rewards for a good study session. It'll keep you fresh and make you want to keep working. If it doesn't come naturally to you, you might even keep a list of fun things to do for ten minutes, such as a major IM session, returning a friend's phone call, playing with a pet, listening to a couple of favorite songs, or playing a game of solitaire—whatever floats your boat. Take a break to do one of these when you sense that you are getting tired. It will help you return energized to your studying for just a little longer.

Getting Extra Help

If you have set your goals high, there may come a time when you feel you have done as much as you can on your own and would like access to an outside "word expert" to help you tackle learning a huge number of words in a logical way. There are several ways to go about this. First, though, talk to your parents and teachers and let them know how serious you are about spelling study and that you feel you need extra help to progress. Perhaps they can help you design a more ambitious and challenging study program and coach you themselves. If no one feels prepared to take on the role of spelling coach, someone may know another teacher, a local college professor, or a graduate student in English or linguistics who would be willing to coach you one or more times per week, either out of the goodness of his or her heart or at a price you and your family can afford.

adobo
antipasto
arugula
biscuit
brochette
calamari
carbonara
chimichanga
colcannon
collation
dashi
delicatessen
flummery
hibachi
hollandaise
kugel
mousse
napoleon
paprika
piccata
pistachio
porringer
preprandial
provender
samosa
seder
spaghetti
stroganoff
succotash
tahini
wasabi
zucchini

When in Doubt, Envision It Out

" I did run into several words I had not studied or seen before the bees in which I participated. After many years of thinking about rules for spelling, I know a few, but at that time I used mostly intuition: I formed a mental picture of how I thought the word was spelled, a sort of theory or 'best guess,' and then spelled it. That's not blind luck, because I had pumped my brain full of words, and my brain unconsciously recognized patterns."

—JACQUES BAILLY,
*1980 National
Spelling Bee champion
(winning word:
elucubrate)*

If you feel you need a boost, but still want to work on your own, you may want to purchase spelling bee software or access to an interactive Web site. There is no need to spend a lot of money on spelling bee preparation unless you wish to do so—many people think you'll learn and retain more if you use your own practice methods, develop your own study lists, and spend your money on reference books you can use in school and at work for years to come—but there are some commercial spelling bee preparation products available, and one of them may be a very effective tool for you. Do an online search for "spelling bee software" and see what you find. Many of the spelling-tutor or "learn to spell" programs that you will see listed will be too elementary for your purposes, so be careful to check that what you are buying is for advanced spelling bee preparation.

Before you buy any program or Web site access, deter-mine whether or not the software will run on your computer and that it is easy to

use. Search for user reviews of the software (not just on the company's Web site) to see how other spellers rate the product. To do your research thoroughly, go to the company's Web site and call the telephone number listed at the

"Contact Us" link. Ask the contact person at the company how long the software or Web site has been available and what evidence he or she can provide of customer success and satisfaction. Make sure you will get good value for the money you spend.

V-I-S-U-A-L-I-Z-E.

Study Tools

If you have access to a computer, go to www.spellingbee.com, the official Web site of the National Spelling Bee, and start clicking. When you find out how great this site is for word study, you might even want to make it your home page. Carolyn's Corner includes tips

Read. Rinse. Repeat.

Good readers make good spellers, and one of the hallmarks of good readers is that they would rather be reading than not. When they're in the shower and there's nothing else available, they'll read the shampoo bottle. So read the ingredients of everything, because it sometimes pays off! Here are a few words that have gone straight from product packaging to the finals of the Scripps National Spelling Bee:

alkaline	emollient	lavender	quassia
antihistamine	enzyme	linseed	serum
arnica	eucalyptus	marjoram	silica
betony	exfoliative	marshmallow	surfactant
borage	glyceride	myrrh	verbena
chrysanthemum	henna	naphtha	wasabi
citronella	hibiscus	petroleum	whorlywort
desiccant	juniper	potassium	yarrow
echinacea	laurel	pyrethrum	yucca

that are frequently updated from September to May. Some of the words discussed there are difficult, but the discussions are easy to understand. There are many advanced spelling tips for spellers who have won school and local bees and are moving on to regional and national finals.

The "Study Resources" link on the www.spellingbee.com home page leads to two of the best free tools at your disposal:

- **Merriam-Webster's *A Dictionary of Prefixes, Suffixes, and Combining Forms.*** This is a sixty-two-page PDF file that shows information for most of the prefixes, suffixes, and combining forms in the Scripps National Spelling Bee's official dictionary, *Webster's Third New*

International Dictionary, Unabridged.
If you watch the National Spelling Bee
on television, you can always tell which
spellers have used this—they're the
ones who ask ques-
tions like, "Does this
word contain the
Latin combining
form *pari-,* meaning
'equal'?" If you want
to be well prepared
for difficult words,
this is the way to go.

- **Consolidated Word List.**
  This is a compilation of more than one
  hundred Scripps National Spelling Bee
  word lists dating as far back as 1950.
  There are more than 20,000 words
  listed, with parts of speech, language
  origins, pronunciations, definitions,
  and sentences provided for more than
  half of them. Many of the words at
  local and regional spelling bees, as well
  as at the National Spelling Bee, appear
  on this list. It is shown as a series of
  PDF files.

  If you're serious about progressing to the
National Spelling Bee finals in Washington,
D.C., you should study these two documents
thoroughly. It's handier to study them on the
computer than on a printout, because they are
automatically searchable. If you don't have a
computer to use at home, you can ask a teacher,

Spell for Love

"I see that kids who have
done well in the past
relish the words they are
learning about. As athletes
are told to 'play for love of
the game,' I tell spellers to
'spell for the love of words.'
Find someone who will be
able to ask you lists of words
and work with this person
consistently. My mother was
my coach. A teacher or a
close friend helped as
well. Make sure you use
Webster's Third. Above all,
believe that you can win. I
was a supposed 'underdog,'
having ranked 81st in my
previous year of competition.
It's all about attitude!"

—NUPUR LALA,
*1999 National Spelling
Bee champion*
(winning word: **logorrhea**)

The Human Body

LEVEL: Intermediate

adductor
anthropometry
auricle
auriform
carcinoma
chromosomal
cilium
clavicle
cochlea
corpuscle
cutaneous
enteritis
febrile
fibrillation
ganglion
humerus
larynx
lumbago
lymph
palate
pancreatic
paralysis
patella
pericardial
peristalsis
physique
podology
pulmonary
tibia
trachea
tricuspid
venous
ventricle

principal, or librarian for extended study time on a school or library computer.

Old Spelling Bee Lists and Study Booklets

Some of the best study tools are lists from earlier spelling bees and old National Spelling Bee study booklets. Over the years, the Scripps National Spelling Bee has produced several series of spelling study booklets. The first, *Words of the Champions,* was used until 1995. Words in *Words of the Champions* were grouped in three categories according to difficulty, and within each category, words were listed in alphabetical order. This booklet was replaced in 1995 by *Paideia,* in which words were categorized according to theme and grouped according to difficulty. If you have older siblings who studied for the spelling bee, you've probably seen a copy of *Paideia,* which contained about 4,000 words. It was discontinued in 2006; and the new study booklet, *Spell It!,* took its place.

The older study booklets are very useful, especially when you are competing at a high level. It is worth trying to borrow these from older students who may have used them in previous years. They may also be cataloged in your school library, so check with your librarian. Occasionally, they are even sold on eBay!

Some of the best advice always comes from someone who's been where you want to be. Scattered throughout this book are forty-five years worth of great spelling and life wisdom from some finalists and national champions.

CHAPTER 4

Roots, Branches, Trees, and Forest

How many languages do you think are spoken in the world today—100, 500, 1,000? Try **6,912**—from Aari, a language of southern Ethiopia, to Zyphe, spoken in Myanmar. Two-thirds of them have no written representation and thus no spelling, but that hasn't stopped the English language from spending the last fifteen centuries borrowing words from around the world.

Roots and Branches

If we imagine the world's languages as a great forest, one of the biggest trees in it would be the Indo-European family of languages, which includes English and most other modern European languages. The tree's trunk is a proto–Indo-European language spoken many thousands of years ago, around 5000 B.C.—long before recorded history. From that ancient tongue grew the Romance languages, such as French, Spanish, and Portuguese; the Germanic languages, including English; the Indo-Iranian languages, such as Sanskrit, Urdu, and Farsi; the Balto-Slavic languages, such as Russian, Polish, and Czech; the Celtic languages, such as Welsh, Breton, and Irish Gaelic; the Hellenic language, which became modern Greek; Albanian; Armenian; and a few other now extinct language groups, such as Anatolian, Thracian, and Illyrian. The Germanic, Romance, and Hellenic branches have contributed heavily to modern English.

The Germanic branch began as a common language about 3,000 years ago. After a thousand years, that language split into several subgroups: East Germanic, North Germanic, and West Germanic. No remnant of East Germanic remains today, but North Germanic is the ancestor of the

What Are "Roots" and How Do You Study Them?

For our purposes, the word *root* has two meanings. It is the English base word from which we derive new words by adding prefixes, suffixes, or inflectional endings or substitutions—like the verb *tell,* which becomes *tells, telling,* and *told,* as well as *retell.* (Inflectional endings or substitutions are the letters you use to change the form of a part of speech, as when making a noun plural or conjugating a verb.)

More important to competitive spellers, the word *root* can also mean an element that is common to all the words of a group, such as *-gnostic* in *gnostic, agnostic,* and *diagnostic.* It may be all or most of what we call a "combining form," which is a word or part of a word borrowed from another language that helps us form new words in English. In the example above, *-gnostic* is a combining form that comes from Greek and means "knowing" or "characterized by knowledge." Few English words come from unique forms, unrelated to any other English word— most are derived from combining forms that are common to many words. That's why they're important to study.

Think of it this way: If spelling bees were adventure video games, combining forms would be the keys that would unlock the doors to the mystery words and get you closer to the trophy.

The National Spelling Bee worked with Merriam-Webster to create an excellent free resource, *A Dictionary of Prefixes, Suffixes, and Combining Forms.* It is posted as a PDF file on the National Spelling Bee Web site, www.spellingbee.com. The entries in this dictionary have been taken from *Webster's Third New International Dictionary* and put into a much easier form to help you study. It's probably the best freebie you'll run across in your quest for spelling excellence.

A Short History of the English Language

A.D. 476 **The Roman Empire falls; Jutes, Angles, and Saxons take over what is now Great Britain and bring their Germanic language along, crowding the Celtic languages into the corners of the British Isles.**

St. Augustine brings Christianity to England and with it many words from Latin.

Vikings whittle away Anglo-Saxon strongholds in Angleland (England) and eventually establish a kingdom and an influence on the language.

Viking ships brought a whole new set of words to the English language.

modern Scandinavian languages of Danish, Norwegian, Swedish, and Icelandic. West Germanic eventually became modern German, Dutch, Flemish, Frisian (English's closest living relative), and English.

The Queen's English (and How We Colonials "Improved" It)

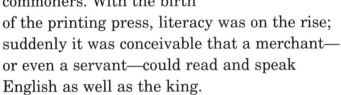

The phrases "the Queen's English" and "the King's English" arose in the sixteenth century with the idea that the monarch's use of written and spoken English should be a model for the language of the commoners. With the birth of the printing press, literacy was on the rise; suddenly it was conceivable that a merchant—or even a servant—could read and speak English as well as the king.

Jolly good, but at the same time, adventuresome Europeans were beginning to show an interest in the New World. As the English populated the American colonies, they adopted many native American and New World Spanish words for things that had been unknown in Europe, such as *tobacco, potato, muskrat, toboggan,* and *hammock.* Even the vocabulary of the upper-class colonists—the ones who were able to speak as well as the king—was changing, becoming quite different from that used in the mother-land. It was becoming distinctly "American."

By 1783, American English had been thriving and changing for more than 150 years, a fact that did not escape Noah Webster, a Yale-educated schoolmaster from a middle-class family. Webster disliked the fact that the schoolbooks he used for teaching were published in England. He believed that American children should learn to read, write, and spell from American books—and not have to go around saying "Cheerio" all the time—so he decided to publish a new series of textbooks. In 1783, Webster's *A Grammatical Institute of the English Language,* more popularly known as the *Blue-Backed Speller,* was published. It was an immediate success and has never been out of print since! (Go ahead and look it up

1066 The Norman Conquest of England makes Norman French popular among the English upper class.

1337–1453 The Hundred Years' War between England and France precipitates the decline of French influence in England.

1348–49 The Black Plague kills more than 30 percent of England's population; the surviving members of the working class are in such demand that, within a few years, their wages rise sharply, giving them greater power, and their language—English—even more influence.

"*In my salad days, I added 1,700 words and phrases to the English language.***"**

1362 First official recognition of English is enacted in Parliament.

1474 William Caxton produces the first book printed in English, *The Recuyell of the Historyes of Troye.*

Webster was a radical believer in simplified spelling: He argued for the omission of all silent letters.

1564–1616 **Shakespeare adds more than 1,700 popular words and phrases to the English language during his lifetime (like *bump, frugal, monumental, salad days,* and *too much of a good thing*) by reviving old words, making nouns from verbs, putting two words together to make a new word, and creating English words from Greek and Latin roots.**

The King James Bible—the classic example of early modern English—is published.

1755 **Samuel Johnson (above) publishes his popular *Dictionary of the English Language* in London.**

1806 **Noah Webster publishes the first American dictionary, followed in 1828 by an even bigger one.**

online—it's available at many bookstores.) By the mid-1800s, it was selling a million copies per year and came in handy for those newfangled contests—called "spelling bees"—that more and more Americans seemed to enjoy.

But Noah Webster knew that American English lacked standard pronunciations and spellings, so he began to develop the first comprehensive American dictionary. Webster was a radical believer in simplified spelling: He argued for the omission of all silent letters. He didn't manage to popularize that idea, but he did establish what we now think of as American spelling—*color* instead of *colour, music* instead of *musick,* and so forth. He also brought the words that everyday Americans used for their tools, food, geography, and indigenous plants and animals firmly into the English language at last. Webster's magnum opus, *An American Dictionary of the English Language,* was published in 1828.

What would Noah Webster make of the language we speak and write today? Can you imagine what he would think of the following paragraph from a newspaper story?

Meanwhile, the space-junk problem is getting worse as the terrestrial world becomes more and more reliant on the sky: We increasingly depend on satellites for duties as diverse as cell-phone calls, TV broadcasting, military reconnaissance and guided hikes by global positioning systems. Satellites are used to track robotic minisubs in Antarctica and animals in the wild.

—Keay Davidson, "Space: The Final Junkyard," *San Francisco Chronicle*, March 12, 2006

Satellites, cell phones, broadcasting, robots, submarines, and global positioning systems were not only unknown in 1828, but didn't even exist until well into the twentieth century—and only a very small part of the Antarctic continent had been spotted in the 1820s. It's easy to see why the dictionary is updated from time to time.

Still, Webster understood that a living language is constantly changing to suit the needs of its speakers, so it's likely that he would be pleased to see how many new words

(continued on page 62)

O ddly enough, the word *newfangled* is a really old word in English. It comes from two Middle English words, *newe*, meaning "new," and *fangel*, which itself comes from an Old English word, *fangen*, meaning "taken."

"*I must be* heard *on the subject of* silent *letters!***"**

And Now a Word from Our Pronouncer . . .

W*e asked Dr. Brian Sietsema, a pronunciation expert (who also happens to be the National Spelling Bee's associate pronouncer) to explain some of the basics of English pronunciation. This was his reply:*

Experts in human speech—linguists—use the term **phoneme** for the idea of a single sound in a given language. A phoneme can be spelled by one letter or a group of letters. Phonemes are often indicated in a special way, using slant marks and letters from different alphabets. For example, the phoneme /t/ expresses the idea of the "t" sound of English in the words *toot, stoop, later,* and *hit* (even though there are slight differences in the way your mouth produces the /t/ among these words).

In purely physical terms, the sounds spelled with the underlined *t* in each of those words are each a different sound, or **phone,** to use the precise linguistic label. The *t* at the beginning of *toot* is produced with a significant puff of air, unlike the *t* of *stoop.* You can convince yourself of this difference by draping a tissue in front of your mouth as you pronounce the two words. The *t* of *stoop* is hardly distinguishable from

a *d;* at normal rates of speaking, almost no one would notice if you were saying "sdoop" rather than *stoop.*

The *t* in *later* is a kind of consonant that linguists call a "flap" or a "tap": It is formed by the tip of the tongue giving a swift tap on the roof of the mouth. This *t* is the same as the sound of the *d* in *ladder.*

At normal rates of speaking in most dialects of English, the *t* in *hit* is completely different from the rest. Whereas the others are formed somewhere near the front of the mouth with the tip of the tongue involved, this *t,* in a phrase like "hit my hand," is formed by a closure back in the throat, with no involvement of the tongue tip. Linguists call this kind of consonantal sound a "glottal stop."

Each of these phones is formed in different ways by the vocal organs in the mouth and throat, and they produce sound waves that are different from one another. While each of these sounds is spelled with the letter *t,* linguists would use a different character to indicate each phone: [tʰ] for *toot,* [t] for *stoop,* [ɾ] for *later,* and [ʔ] for hit. (Notice that phones are enclosed in square brackets, but phonemes in slashes.)

As speakers of English, we regard these different phones as being really just the expression of a single category of sound, the English phoneme /t/. In our language, therefore, [tʰ], [t], [ɾ], and [ʔ] are all allophones of the phoneme /t/. Speakers of other languages, however, may regard these phones as being distinct kinds of sound which are therefore to be spelled with different letters. Speakers of Hindi, for example, hear a clear distinction between [tʰ] and [t], and for them this difference makes for a difference in meaning. For them, these two phones belong to two different phonemes, /th/ and /t/. Speakers of Arabic, on the other hand, perceive the phones [p] and [b] as being essentially one and the same kind of sound, i.e., allophones of a single phoneme /p/; in English we regard [p] and [b] as expressions of two distinct phonemes /p/ and /b/ that consequently make for a difference in meaning, as in *pat* and *bat.*

A familiar example of how phones are perceived differently in different languages comes from comparing English and Spanish. In English, *den* and *then* begin with two different sounds, [d] and [ð], which are regarded as two distinct phonemes. In Spanish, however, these two sounds are both perceived as allophones of the Spanish phoneme /d/. These allophones occur in different phonetic contexts: [d] is found at the beginning of a word, but [ð] after a vowel, as in the phrase *de nada,* which to English speakers sounds like "day nah-thah."

Samir Patel asks for languages of origin.

Transliteration, or How Do You Spell *sushi* in Japanese?

English words use the Roman or Latin alphabet, which is one of many alphabets. English has borrowed words from many languages, some of which use, or used, a different alphabet, but when we bring these words into English, we use our alphabet to represent them. The technical term for this process is *transliteration*. English words from Greek, Arabic, Japanese, Russian, Sanskrit, and many other languages have been transliterated.

and phrases American English has adopted since he published his dictionary—although it's hard to say if he'd be happy about *aerobicize, mall rat,* or the fact that *bad* can now mean "good."

Hey, Get Your Hands off My Nouns!

What do a ferret and the English language have in common? Both love to steal and stash whatever they can. The English language has a penchant for picking the pockets of other languages. Most of the words in the English language, in fact, belonged originally to other languages.

Languages often have signature spelling patterns for various sounds. You probably already know several of these patterns. The word *tortilla* looks and sounds Spanish, and the word *ballet* looks and sounds French. Knowing some spelling patterns associated with various languages has helped many spellers in competition. If a word is pronounced for you, and you are told the word's language of origin, your chances of ferreting out the correct spelling are much better.

So let's visit a few languages and take a look at some of the signature spellings of various sounds.

Latin

Some sources indicate that almost 30 percent of the most commonly used English words have Latin in their history. Some students of Latin think of it as a difficult subject, but its spelling patterns are very consistent. As you learn to spell several words that have Latin as the language of origin, you gain a "feel" for how all words from Latin are spelled. Latin has few surprises.

Some notable sounds and spellings:

LATIN

SOUND (what you hear)	SPELLING (what you often see)	EXAMPLES
long *e* at end of plural noun	*ae*	algae, larvae, antennae (Note: Many of these words can also be pronounced with a long *i*.)
long *i* at end of plural noun	*i*	magi, fungi, cacti, alumni (Note: Some of these words can also be pronounced with a long *e*.)
"oo" as in *ooze*	*u*	recluse, revolution, nucleus, rumor, affluent, ruin
/y/ + "oo" as in *ooze*	*u*	commute, acute, municipal, nucleus, diffuse, tunic, deduce, cumulus
/y/ + schwa ("yuh")	*u*	deciduous, cellular, cumulus, argument, accurate
/gz/	*x*	exist, exhume, auxiliary, exaggerate, exonerate, exhaust, examine
/k/	c	candidate, execute, proclaim, constitution, college, locate, facsimile

The Letter of the Law

"I stuck with Latin throughout high school. In college, I majored in Latin and spent a semester in Rome. For a couple of years, I was a Teach for America fifth-grade teacher and a stickler for proper spelling; then I went to law school. There's no particular link in my mind between lawyering and spelling, but I did find studying for the bar strangely reminiscent of studying for the bee. I also think that surviving a spelling bee, or any other middle-school public performance, helps reduce kids' stage fright and public speaking anxiety when they go on to try other things."

—AMANDA GOAD, *1992 National Spelling Bee champion* (winning word: **lyceum**)

Notes on Latin Spellings

Most of the time, / s / is spelled *s* in words of Latin origin. Sometimes, however, / s / is spelled *sc: muscle, rescind, descend, adolescent.*

The letter *z* is rare in words of Latin origin.

The letters *k* and *w* do not exist in English words of Latin origin unless the words have passed through another language before coming into English.

Because Latin words have no *rh*'s, *ph*'s, and *ch*'s—unless the Latin word got them from Greek—English words of Latin origin will not usually have *rh, ph,* or *ch* in their spellings.

Most of the time / m / at the end of a word of Latin origin is spelled *m*. Sometimes, however, it is spelled *mb: aplomb, bomb, plumb.*

Sometimes / n / at the end of a word of Latin origin is spelled *gn: design, benign, impugn, align, assign.*

The letter *i* is a vowel often used to connect two Latin word elements. If the connecting vowel sound is a schwa and you must guess at the spelling of this sound, the letter *i* might be a good guess: *flor**i**sugent, matr**i**monial, ov**i**form, ped**i**form, bacill**i**form, bil**i**rubin, manicure, ren**i**form.*

Greek is frequently viewed as the language of science.

Greek

reek is frequently viewed as the language
of science. Because many good spelling
bee words have definitions that relate to
the various sciences, it is important for spellers
to explore this language of origin and to learn
its signature in words.

Some notable sounds and spellings are:

GREEK

SOUND (what you hear)	SPELLING (what you often see)	EXAMPLES
/f/	*ph*	alphabet, phase, philosophy, phonics, telegraph, diphtheria, phobia, amphibian, sphere
short *i*	*y*	abyss, dyslexia, synonym, sympathy, system, gymnasium, odyssey, Olympiad, onyx, syzygy
/k/	*c, k,* or *ch*	carcinogen, cathode, democracy, kinetic, krypton, kaumographer, kaleidoscope, chrome, chloride, chaos, echo, chorus, technology, architect, character
/r/	*r/rh/rrh*	parallel, periphery, theory, pyramid, thorax, rheostat, rhapsody, rhinoceros, rhythm, hemorrhage, cirrhosis
/z/ at beginning of word	*x* (from Greek letter *xi*)	xylophone, xanthic, xenial
/z/ at beginning of word	*z* (from Greek letter *zeta*)	zeal, zephyr, zetetic, zeugma

The Kiss of Success

"I recall telling ESPN that I knew all of my words when they asked me in front of the camera. It was because I felt I had known all of them instinctively, even though I hadn't previously encountered two of the words, **poimenics** and **bouchon**. What helped me arrive at the spelling of **bouchon** so quickly was that I had studied spelling patterns from Romance languages extensively. When Dr. Cameron gave me the proper French pronunciation, it clicked immediately and I had no trouble spelling the word. With **poimenics**, I used the 'Keep It Simple for Success' (KISS) rule. I just trusted my intuition on the word and didn't allow myself to stray from it. None of the clues given were helpful to me, but I just asked repeatedly for the pronunciation and tried to develop a feel for the word. It worked!"

—NUPUR LALA,
*1999 National
Spelling Bee champion*

Notes on Greek Spellings

There are many ways to spell the same Greek sound in English. For example, /th/ can be spelled *th*, *phth*, and *chth* and /n/ can be spelled *n*, *gn*, *pn*, *mn*, and *cn*. Greek is full of surprises!

The long *u* can be spelled *u*, *eu*, and *ou*. If a word from Greek can be pronounced with an optional /y/ in front of a long *u* sound (as in *neurology*), or if the long *u* comes after /s/ (as in *pseudonym*), it is likely to be spelled *eu*. With Greek food words like *moussaka* and *souvlaki*, the long *u* is usually spelled *ou*.

While *y* is a telltale Greek spelling of a short *i*, the short *i* can also be spelled *i* in words of Greek origin: *hippopotamus, arithmetic, trichotillomania*. The letter *y* can also be used to spell a long *i*: *hygiene, cryogen, myelocyte*.

The letter *o* is the vowel most often used to connect two Greek word elements. If the connecting vowel sound is a schwa and you must guess at the spelling of this sound, the letter *o* is a very good guess: *xylophone, carcinogen, electrolyte, homonym, octopod, economist, atmosphere, geometric, gyroscope, hypnotist*.

Learning the meaning and spelling of Greek word elements takes the mystery out of many scientific words.

Of the words most commonly used in English, as many have French in their histories as have Latin.

English

ome sources indicate that around one fourth of the words in the English language were "born" as English words, but these represent a very large proportion of words we use in writing and speaking. Words whose origin is English are many of our basic, everyday words. Because of their familiarity, they are easy for us to spell—even if their spelling includes silent letters. Words such as *knowledge* and *writing* give us little trouble because we have seen and used them for almost as long as we can remember.

Generally speaking, though, words that have English as the language of origin do not contain tricky letter combinations. The safest approach to spelling a mystery word whose language of origin is English is to spell it exactly as it sounds, if no other clues are available.

French

f all the modern foreign languages that can be spotted in English words, French is *premier*. Of the words most commonly used in English, as many have French in their histories as have Latin. Do not, under any *circumstance,* be *insouciant* about the impact of French on spelling!

Some notable sounds and spellings are shown on the chart on the next pages:

Advice en français

s you are *en route* to the top, it might be *une bonne idée* to try to develop a certain *sangfroid* toward the audience.

FRENCH

SOUND (what you hear)	SPELLING (what you often see)	EXAMPLES
long *a*	*e* or *é*	carburetor, elite, regime, dégringolade, decoupage, demarche, fete
long *a*	*ez*	suivez, rendezvous, oyez
long *a* at end of word	*et*	sachet, crochet, duvet, parquet, beignet, gourmet, chalet, ricochet, buffet, ballet, valet, piolet
long *a* at end of word	*e/ee* or *é/ée*	café, macrame, abbé, entrée, matinee, melee
/y/ + long *a* at end of word	*ier*	dossier, costumier, atelier, cahier, espalier, métier, pompier, tapissier, douanier
long *e* at end of word	*ee*	fricassee, marquee
long *e* at end of word	*ie*	papeterie, japonaiserie, bourgeoisie, menagerie, bijouterie, minauderie, jalousie, batterie, gaucherie, gaminerie, coterie, fourberie, sortie
long *i*	*aille*	rocaille, trouvaille, grisaille
long *o*	*aut*	auteur, soubresaut, hauteur, sauterne
long *o*	*eau*	eau, beau, trousseau, nouveau, chapeau, gateau, jambeau, plateau, heaume
long *o*	*eaux* (plural of words ending in -*eau*)	bordereaux, tableaux, Watteaux, morceaux
long *o*	*au*	mauve, taupe, paupiette, gaufrette, soubresaut

SOUND	SPELLING	EXAMPLES
(what you hear)	*(what you often see)*	
/et/	*ette*	banquette, estafette, layette, croquette, fanchonette, blanquette, lorgnette, noisette, marionette, pirouette
		(Note: There are many words, such as *baronet, motet, annulet, coronet, flageolet, martinet,* and *bayonet,* that do not have the *-ette* spelling for /et/.)
"ahzh" at end of word	*age*	fuselage, garage, camouflage, sabotage, dressage, bavardage, espionage, persiflage, barrage, montage, maquillage, triage, vernissage
"odd" at end of word	*ade*	facade, croustade, ballade, chamade, persillade, glissade, roulade, levade
"air" at end of word	*aire*	doctrinaire, billionaire, legionnaire, solitaire, luminaire
"oo" as in *ooze*	*ou*	soufflé, boudoir, coup, bouquet, loupe, boutique, rouge, soubriquet, bouffant, bouillon, moulage, tourlourou, bijou, froufrou, rouleau
"oo" as in *ooze*	*u*	fondu, ecru, fichu, impromptu, menu, ormolu, parvenu, tutu
"oo" as in *ooze*	*ieu*	lieu, bondieuserie, purlieu, lieutenant, milieu
/sh/ at beginning of word	*ch*	chagrin, chablis, chevaline, chaise
/sh/ at beginning of word	*sh*	shallot, shalloon, shako, shagreen

FRENCH

SOUND (what you hear)	SPELLING (what you often see)	EXAMPLES
/sh/ at end of word	*che*	gobemouche, brioche, cache, demarche, gauche, louche, panache, quiche, seiche, parfleche, potiche
/k/ at end of word	*que*	antique, grotesque, cinque, technique, mosque, arabesque, boutique, pique, claque, roque, clique
/g/ at end of word	*gue*	gigue, vogue, morgue, intrigue, fugue, fatigue, colleague, plague
"el" at end of word	*elle*	gazelle, mademoiselle, nacelle, belle, chandelle, jumelle (Note: A few words, like *noel* and *morel,* are spelled *el.*)
schwa + /l/	*el*	bevel, estoppel, camel, cancel, caramel, enamel, gravel, kennel
/w/ + "oz"	*oise*	ardoise, dacquoise, bourgeoise, nicoise, reboise, genoise
/n/ + /y/	*gn*	beignet, rognon, chignon, espagnole, vigneron, guignol, vignette, poignant, lorgnette, seigneur, champignon
/n/ + /w/	*gnoi*	baignoire, peignoir
schwa + /r/	*eur*	friseur, persifleur, jongleur, auteur, flaneur, fleuron, tiqueur (See note on *-er/-re* and *-or/-our* below.)
"il" at end of word	*ille*	coquille, escadrille, quadrille

Notes on French Spelling

French, true to its Latin heritage, tends to use *c* and avoid *k* for spelling the /k/ sound.

One of Noah Webster's goals was to simplify the spelling of English words by making them more similar in appearance to the way that they sound.

Many words from French have silent consonants. Examples include *maillot, debut, picot, griot, ouvert* (silent *t*); *debris, Franglais, patois, coulis, apropos* (silent *s*); *champagne, bersagliere* (silent *g*); *roux, faux, bordereaux* (silent *x*); *coup* (silent *p*); *sangfroid* (silent *d*), and *email* (silent *l*—and it's French for "enamel").

O ver the past several years, the French word *connoisseur* has been the most frequently used word on Scripps National Spelling Bee word lists.

A nasal vowel ("honk, honk") can be spelled many ways in English words of French origin. The nasal vowel results in various silent consonants:

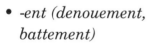

- *-ent (denouement, battement)*
- *-ant (croissant, dansant)*
- *-on (frisson, garçon)*
- *-emps (contretemps)*
- *-in (boudin, baragouin)*
- *-en- (tendu, malentendu)*
- *-em- (croquembouche, embonpoint)*
- *-oint (embonpoint)*

One of Noah Webster's goals was to simplify the spelling of English words by making them more similar in appearance to the way that they sound. With words from French ending in schwa + /r/, such as *theatre* and *centre* and *colour* and *glamour,* he tried hard to change their spellings to *theater/center* and *color/glamor.* Many words were already firmly established in English, however, so what we have now are two acceptable spellings of each word. Some words such as *massacre* and *ogre* were so firmly established that they have only the traditional French spelling.

The *oi* letter combination is seen in many words of French origin and has many different sounds. Familiarize yourself with the sound and

2005 Scripps National Spelling Bee champion Anurag Kashyap, from San Diego, California, autographs another speller's hand.

Except for a few consonants, words from Spanish are often spelled just as you would think they should be.

spelling of words such as *foible, adroit, renvoi, moiré, chinoiserie, boudoir, coiffure, grimoire, avoirdupois, connoisseur, porpoise,* and *mademoiselle.*

Spanish

nglish words from Spanish have very consistent spelling and the patterns are easy to memorize. Except for a few consonants (like *ll,* which sounds like /y/, and *j,* which sounds like /h/), words from Spanish are often spelled just as you would think they should be. If you are at the microphone and are asked to spell a mystery word of Spanish origin, it's best to spell it as it sounds. For example, if the final sound is a long *o,* spell it with an *o.* Don't pull out the French *-eau.* Don't try to put a fancy spin on the spelling of words from Spanish!

Some notable sounds and spellings are in the table on the next page.

The Spanish alphabet does not contain a *k.* The letter *k* is found in English words from Spanish only when Spanish has borrowed those words from some other language.

Don't use *ph* to spell the /f/ sound in English words from Spanish.

With the exception of *ll* and *rr,* double letters in words of Spanish origin are uncommon.

Foreign Study Tips

Go to the library and find dictionaries or textbooks for other unusual foreign languages that use a Roman alphabet, such as Welsh, Gaelic, or Basque. Peruse them to see if any spelling patterns surface and check the pronunciations. This might give you a hint for spelling unusual words that have come from these languages to English.

If you have an electronic dictionary with a search feature, you can use it to search for all the words that have a particular language of origin. Look at each list of words from a given language and see if you can spot spelling patterns within this language.

SPANISH

SOUND (what you hear)	SPELLING (what you often see)	EXAMPLES
long *a*	*e*	ceja, rejoneador, zarzuela, coleta, capeador, sevillana
/g/ + long *a*	*gue*	vargueno, malaguena
long *a* at end of word	*e* or *é*	suerte, padre, atole, baile, compadre, guanche, infante, jarabe, olé, jefe, molave, norte, pinche, sucre, tiple, hombre, amole, bisagre
long *e* at end of word	*i*	bonaci, Bribri, caji, guazuti, houvari, javali, mani, macabi, tecali, zemi, aguaji
long *e* at end of word	*e*	vigilante, amole, adobe, bisagre, casabe, cenote, jinete, chapote, chayote, mole, monte, pinole, rosinante, timbe, Apache, hombre
long *e* followed by "yuh"/"yoh"	*illa/illo*	banderilla, mantilla, tortilla, blanquillo, piloncillo, tomatillo
long *o*	*o*	desperado, pronto, rodeo, Latino, amigo, concho, diablo, gazpacho, tango, zocalo
/h/	*j*	jicama, junta, aparejo, rejoneador, jacal
/k/	*c*	cabana, cacao, cordovan, hurricane, cafeteria, cantina
/k/	*qu*	ronquil, quiaquia, quinta, vaquero
"kay"	*que*	quesadilla, quebrada, quebracho
schwa at end of word	*a*	bonanza, bodega, hacienda, cabana, junta, plaza, fajita, chinchilla

The letters *ch* and *ll* are considered single letters in Spanish. That's why these letter combinations pop up frequently in English words of Spanish origin.

Make lists of words that do not follow the "spell it like it sounds" guideline: for example, *tilde* (final schwa spelled with *e*).

A /th/ sound will be spelled with a *d* if it is surrounded by vowels. Examples: *rejoneador, toreador, cogida, capeador.*

German

Historically, German has had an enormous influence on English, but words that have come from modern German can still look very unusual to us.

Some notable sounds and spellings are shown on the next page.

Notes on German Spelling

German words love *k*'s, *ck*'s, and *ch*'s. They avoid *c*'s, except when the German word is borrowed from Greek or some other language that has an unusual preference for *c*'s. Remember: The letter *c* rarely appears alone in words of German origin; you'll almost always see it paired with *k* as in *glockenspiel*, or *h* as in *geistlich*.

The Guttural /kh/

The German *ch* is often pronounced with a little gargle in the back of the throat. Try saying the word *book*. Now say it again—but this time, when you pronounce the *k*, allow your throat to stay slightly open and push a small amount of air through. This guttural sound is also present in other languages like Yiddish and Russian, though English often changes its pronunciation in adopted words to a safe, boring /k/.

GERMAN

SOUND (what you hear)	SPELLING (what you often see)	EXAMPLES
long *e*	*ie*	vorspiel, glockenspiel, kunstlied, kriegspiel, blitzkrieg, volkslied, zwieback, wienerwurst, wiesenboden
long *i*	*ei*	abseil, Fahrenheit, gesundheit, gauleiter, leitmotiv, einkanter, gneiss, zeitgeist, Kneippism, schwarmerei, meister, ortstein, geige, poltergeist
/ch/ and /sh/	*sch*	affenpinscher, gegenschein, schottische, kitsch, Nietzschean, schnitzel, putsch, austausch, bergschrund
"lick" (sort of!)	*lich*	geistlich, lieblich, schlich, frohlich (See sidebar on the guttural /kh/.)
/v/	*w*	wenzel, edelweiss, wisent, weltpolitik, Weimaraner, wedel, leberwurst, wiesenboden
/k/	*k*	einkorn, katzenjammer, einkanter, kohlrabi, lebkuchen, blitzkrieg, kipfel, randkluft, kuchen, nachtmusik, kitsch, steinkern, weltpolitik
/k/	*ck*	pickelhaube, schnecke, zwieback, pumpernickel
/k/	*ch*	echt

A Spelling Glitch

"At the 1980 national finals, when the competition was reduced to two spellers—Jacques Bailly and me—I was asked to spell **glitch**. *Glitch*, of course, means 'a mistake,' and it entered the English language with the space industry in the 1960s and became a commonly used word with the advent of personal computer usage in the 1980s. But in 1980 very few people had computers on their desks at work or in their homes, so *glitch* was not yet a common word. So, when I was asked to spell this simple-sounding word at the end of the Bee, I instantly thought that there must be a trick spelling. Then the pronouncer offered that its origin was German, and that bit of information confirmed my hunch that the spelling was g-l-i-t-s-c-h. I was wrong, of course, and the rest is history: Jacques Bailly corrected my misspelling of *glitch* and went on to spell **elucubrate** to win the Bee. In 1991, soon after being employed by Scripps to help run the National Spelling Bee, I had the privilege of examining the full word list for the 1980 bee. I was able to see that if I had spelled *glitch* correctly, my next word would have been **intonaco**, and I acknowledged that I probably would have misspelled that word, too. I never had any doubt that Jacques Bailly deserved the championship, but having the *intonaco* information helped me feel even better about the way things happened."

—PAIGE PIPKIN KIMBLE,
*1981 National
Spelling Bee champion*

Italian

I talian is a language that has given us many popular spelling bee words for beautiful music and yummy food. Some notable sounds and spellings:

ITALIAN

SOUND (what you hear)	SPELLING (what you often see)	EXAMPLES
long *a* at end of word	*e*	padre, volante, tagliatelle, pappardelle, ballabile, padrone, macrame, principe, scintillante
long *e* at end of word	*i*	spaghetti, salami, macaroni, perciatelli, ziti, Amati, brindisi, cannelloni, cannoli, calamari, literati, Carbonari, ravioli
long *e* at end of word	*e*	minestrone, torrone, fettuccelle, schiavone, brillante, campanile, canzone, pococurante, monte, lazzarone, pallone, panettone
long *e* + long *o* at end of word	*io*	impresario, atrio, punctilio, arpeggio, nuncio, oratorio, pistachio, studio, capriccio, intaglio
long *o* at end of word	*o*	alto, bravo, crescendo, bambino, fiasco, motto, maestro, libretto, largo, ghetto, graffito, inferno, incognito, palmetto, pesto, piano, piccolo, capriccioso, prosciutto, Reggio, soprano, tremolo, zero, amaretto
/y/ + long *o* at end of word	*io*	imbroglio, intaglio, bardiglio, latticinio, preludio, verdicchio
"eenie" at end of word	*ini*	rappini, spiedini, ditalini, spaghettini, zucchini, tortellini

SOUND *(what you hear)*	SPELLING *(what you often see)*	EXAMPLES
/ch/	*cc*	breccia, carpaccio, capriccio, fettuccelle, mostaccioli, focaccia, fettuccine
/k/ before schwa or long *o*	*cc*	beccafico, spiccato, squacco, zocco, zoccolo, zacco, stucco, piccolo
/k/ before schwa, short *a,* or long *o*	*c*	cantata, pecorino, cambio, campanile, magnifico, giocoso, pococurante
/k/ before long *e,* short *e,* or long *a*	*ch*	chianti, chiaroscuro, marchesa
/ts/	*zz*	pizza, intermezzo, mozzarella, palazzo, pizzicato
/ny/	*gn*	agnolotti, signorina, Bolognese, malmignatte
/sk/ before long or short *e*	*sch*	maraschino, scherzo
schwa at end of word	*a*	regatta, bravura, buffa, camorra, durezza, fughetta, saltimbocca, sonatina, toccata, cantata, ocarina, piazza

Watch out for a silent *g* in a few words of Italian origin! Examples include *intaglio, gnocchi,* and *scagliola.*

Italian words seem to avoid using *k* to spell the /k/ sound. Note in the list above the three other ways to spell it!

Japanese Doubles

Only seven words that have come to us directly from Japanese have double consonants:

hokku
issei
momme
seppuku
shikken
tenno
teppanyaki

Japanese

Words from Japanese are relatively new in English, partly because Japan was closed to Western foreigners from the seventeenth through the nineteenth centuries. Now that Japanese culture has gone global, it's good to know some of these words—especially the food words! Some notable sounds and spellings can be found on the facing page.

Turkish

It was **kismet** that Turkish and English would one day meet. Some notable sounds and spellings:

TURKISH

SOUND (what you hear)	SPELLING (what you often see)	EXAMPLES
long *e* at end of word	*i*	vali, Azeri, raki, effendi, kasseri
long *i*	*ai*	taiga, Bairam, serai
/k/	*c*	canun, caza
/k/	*k*	kilim, altilik, kismet, Mamluk, palanka, sanjak, moussaka, kasseri
/k/	*kh*	khagan, khilafat, tarkhan

JAPANESE

SOUND *(what you hear)*	SPELLING *(what you often see)*	EXAMPLES
long *a*	*ei*	reiki, geisha, issei, kibei, nisei, sensei
long *a* at end of word	*e*	yosenabe, urushiye
long *e* at end of word	*i*	Kabuki, odori, hibachi, origami, tsunami, wasabi, zori, Meiji, Romaji, dashi, kanji, awabi, odori, tatami, sashimi, chorogi, fuji, haori, koji, obi, randori, shikii, torii, shogi, sukiyaki, urushi, gi, surimi, sushi, tamari, teriyaki, umami, yakitori
long *e* at end of word	*e*	Kamikaze, momme, mume
long *i*	*ai*	bonsai, yamamai, mai, samurai, banzai, haikai, shintai, aikido, kaiseki
long *o*	*o*	mikado, pachinko, koto, miso, odori, genro, gyokuro, judo, kendo, mondo, sumo, tenno, dojo, zendo, gingko
"oo" as in *ooze* at the end of word	*u*	chanoyu, Bunraku, ayu, kudzu, haiku, hokku, shiatsu, zaibatsu, tofu, ansu, kwazoku, maru, Gagaku
/k/	*k*	kakemono, bugaku, kana, kimono, haiku
schwa at end of word	*a*	ikebana, ama, katana, geisha, sayonara, kana, mana, ninja, soba

Portuguese

The Portuguese have always been sailors, and their language bears traces of their wide travels. Many English words from Portuguese have also passed through non-European languages, such as Sanskrit, Malay, Arabic, and various African tongues. It's important to remember the close relationship of Portuguese and Spanish, because there are many similarities in spelling, but words from Portuguese do have a few distinctive patterns.

PORTUGUESE

SOUND (what you hear)	SPELLING (what you often see)	EXAMPLES
long *a*	*ei*	pareira, copoeira, barbeiro, feijoada, freijo, seringueiro
long *i*	*ai*	caixinha, coaita, pirai, saimiri, caique
long *u*	*u*	teju, munguba, murumuru, pirarucu
long *u*	*o*	choro, chocalho, fado
long *u*	*ou*	cachou, toucan, marabout, chibigouazou
/sh/	*x*	maxixe, paxiuba, abacaxi, caixinha, guaxima, xarque
/sh/ at beginning of word	*ch*	chamade, chamiso, chocalho, chavante
/k/	*c*	candiru, callimico, carambola
/k/	*qu*	quica, jequitiba, macaque
/zh/	*j*	feijoada, teju, acajou

Persian

ost words from Persian go through several languages before entering English, so you may notice some patterns shared by Hindi, Arabic, Turkish, and Sanskrit.

Some notable sounds and spellings are shown in the chart on the next page.

Sanskrit and/or Hindi

any of the words we immediately recognize as coming from the Indian subcontinent are Hindu religious terms such as *yoga, ashram,* and *karma.* However, Sanskrit and Hindi are both Indo-European languages and have donated many more common words to their distant cousin English—words like *pajama, bungalow, brother,* and *jungle.*

Some notable sounds and spellings are shown on the next page.

English words from Sanskrit sometimes contain a silent *h:*

- /t/ can be spelled *th (kathakali)*
- /b/ can be spelled *bh (bhalu)*
- /d/ can be spelled *dh (dharma)*
- /k/ can be spelled *kh (gymkhana)*
- /p/ can be spelled *ph (phansigar)*

Oh, the Horror!

"While I could make educated guesses based on roots for the vast majority of words I could not specifically remember, there remains one that truly confounded me. I remember that in one of the final rounds of the 2000 national finals I was asked to spell **emmetropia.** During the postmortem, I learned that I had been quizzed on it previously, but I had no recollection of it. I quickly closed my eyes and prayed that God would grant me the correct letters for this word. I could recall no rules for spelling it. All I knew was that the spelling *e-m-m-e-t-r-o-p-i-a* made sense, but I remember the horror I experienced as I reflected on the numerous other 'logically correct' spellings. But the chance had to be taken, and I had a sense of peace about the orthography I had chosen."

—GEORGE THAMPY,
*2000 National
Spelling Bee champion*
(winning word:
demarche)

PERSIAN

SOUND *(what you hear)*	SPELLING *(what you often see)*	EXAMPLES
long *e* at end of word	*i*	abbasi, Kabuli, kusti, tangi, Turki
/g/	*g*	idgah
/g/	*gh*	ispaghul, ghorkhar
/k/	*c*	calean, carboy, caravan
/k/	*k*	abkar, kamboh, kusti, Kabuli, karez, kran
/k/	*kh*	Bakhtiari, dakhma, farsakh, ghorkhar, nakhoda

SANSKRIT AND/OR HINDI

SOUND *(what you hear)*	SPELLING *(what you often see)*	EXAMPLES
long *e* at end of word	*i*	Hindi, amani, bibi, basmati, tandoori, begari, chakari, jungli, chhatri, dasturi, dhauri, granthi, kangri, koftgari, Pindari, lassi, poori, roti, pachisi, darzi, sabzi
schwa at end of word	*a*	mahatma, Buddha, karma, natya, chakra, pajama
schwa at end of word	*ah*	almirah, keddah, ayah, khankah, kajawah, numnah
"ana" as in British pronunciation of *banana* (sort of!) at end of word	*ana*	Nirvana, gymkhana, dhyana, jnana, rana, zenana

Miscellaneous Language Tidbits

hese languages don't commonly lend words to English, and the words we do have from them tend to be somewhat unfamiliar. However—hint, hint—they're often good spelling bee words!

In words of Afrikaans origin:

- Familiarize yourself with letter combinations in words such as *uintjie, Uitlander, uitspan, vaalhaai, volksraad, umfaan, aardvark, bobbejaan, geeldikkop, wildebeest, vetkousie.* Make a list of unusual spellings for various sounds.

In words of Arabic origin:

- long *e* is sometimes spelled *ih: mihrab, ihram, faqih, tasbih, Lihyanic*

- many words are spelled more or less as they sound: *mancala, masjid, kemancha, albetad, azoth, bejel*

- there is sometimes a silent *h: madhab, dhimmi, dhikr, dukhn, fellagha*

In words of Eskimo origin:

- /k/ is almost always spelled *k: Eskimo, komatik, manak, kooletah, muktuk, anorak, kamik, makluk, kashim*

- /k/ is sometimes spelled *q: qiviut*

In words of Hawaiian origin:

- there are no silent letters such as the *e* in *hole*

A Beastly Number of Malaysian Words

A number of unusual animal names *(teledu, cobego, cassowary, pangolin, siamang, bruang, gourami, kokam, linsang, lory, musang, simpai, tokay, tangilin)* come to us from the Malay language. Malay is spoken extensively not only in Malaysia, but also in parts of Thailand, Singapore, Brunei, the Philippines, and Borneo. The language is as rich and varied as the animal life in this part of the world—Malay has many dialects and, like English, has borrowed extensively from other languages such as Arabic and Sanskrit.

Your Turn, Gospodin!

During the twentieth century, the Russian language gave English many new words. Some were used for political and social concepts pertaining to the now-defunct Soviet Union: *agitpunkt, agrogorod, apparatchik, cheka, commissar, glasnost, gulag, Kremlin, perestroika, refusenik, samizdat,* and *soviet*. Some were scientific and technical terms: *tokamak, sputnik, cosmonaut,* and even *reflexology*. But many English words from Russian have far older meanings: *steppe, nagaika, samovar, mammoth, kasha, balalaika, sobornost, feldsher, gospodin, troika, purga, babushka, chastushka, tundra*. Notice that there's still something identifiably "Russian" about these words. Look them up, and see if you can figure out some of the typical spelling patterns yourself!

- the only consonants used are *h, k, l, m, n, p,* and *w*
- consonants are never doubled
- the last letter is always a vowel

In words of Hebrew origin:

- a final "ah" sound and a final schwa sound are often spelled *ah:* *bedikah, genizah, menorah, aliyah, takkanah, bamah, amidah, Asherah, neilah, taharah, parashah, gezerah, hashkabah, Jeremiah, kapparah, Jonah, kabbalah, mizpah, messiah*

- double consonants seem relatively common: *hosanna, kibbutz, shibboleth, Gehenna, akkum, kiddush, bikkurim, kapparah, kinnor, gabbai, koppa, messiah, hallel, Perizzite, rabbi, sabbath, shittah, takkanah, viddui*

In words of Hungarian origin:

- /s/ can occasionally be spelled *s* or *tz* but is nearly always *sz: tzigane, Kuvasz, Lisztian, puszta, szaibelyite, veszelyite, szmikite, Szekler*

In words of Polish origin:

- /v/ is usually spelled with a *w: kujawiak, krakowiak*

- /k/ is usually spelled with a *k: kielbasa, babka, oberek*

In words of Russian origin:

- /k/ is usually spelled with a *k: tokamak, apparatchik, zolotnik, bolshevik, chinovnik, gopak, gudok, kulak, obrok,*

Test Your Expertise

Are you etymologically savvy now? Let's find out. Match each word in the left columns to one of the languages on the right. There are two words from Sanskrit, three from Greek, one from Persian, three from Japanese, four from French, three from German, five from Latin, four from Italian, and five from Spanish. Answers are on page 88.

sensor	**piatti**	Sanskrit _____
mythology	**bushido**	Greek _____
penicillin	**flotilla**	_____
ichthyoid	**randori**	Persian _____
graffito	**avalanche**	Japanese _____
simpatico	**badinage**	French _____
enoki	**duende**	_____
alameda	**abduct**	German _____
phosphorus	**Borsalino**	_____
meerschaum	**karuna**	Latin _____
eigenvalue	**antebellum**	_____
tantra	**bonus**	Italian _____
nouveau	**avoirdupois**	_____
quesadilla	**spiel**	Spanish _____
toccata	**percale**	_____

(For more games, see Chapter 7.)

sputnik, kurgan. Note: We have "_ck_'d" some spellings such as _cossack._

- /k/ + schwa is usually spelled _ka_: _babushka, burka, perestroika, balalaika, chastushka, nagaika, troika_

In words of Scandinavian origin:

- Many borrowed Old Norse words contain the consonant group /sk/, which is still spelled _sk_ as it was in Old Norse: _skid, skin, skip, skirl, skirt, skulk, skull, sky._ Other Old Norse words that had the consonant group /sk/ took a detour; when they landed in present day English, their /sk/ sounds were spelled _sc: scab, scale, score, scrape, scowl, scrimp._

Capitalized Words

The Scripps National Spelling Bee began using capitalized words in 1997, which increased the number of good words they had to draw from by several thousand. The National Spelling Bee rules state that the speller need not specify that a letter is capitalized, so there's no need to worry if you get one of these words—as long as you've studied how to spell it! On page 90 you will find just a few of the capitalized words that have appeared in recent National Spelling Bees or on Scripps-published

Neologisms often make excellent spelling bee words.

Neologisms

*N*eologism* is defined in *Webster's Third* as "a new word, usage, or expression." How new a word has to be in order to be considered a neologism is open to debate, but at some point in time, every word in the dictionary has been a neologism! Many neologisms start out as slang, but widespread and frequent use eventually gains them acceptance among linguistic traditionalists. *Note:* Several words below are not listed in *Webster's Third*.

applet
bioprospect
bioremediation
biosolid
bioterror
blog
carjacking
chipotle
cocooning
cohousing
cybercafe
cybernaut
cybrarian
defragmenter
digerati
ecoterrorism
electronica
emoticon

extranet
extremophile
fashionista
filovirus
Frankenfood
gangsta
gelcap
genomics
glasnost
greenwashing
Habanero
heteroglossia
hoodie
hospitalist
hyperlink
hyperther-
    mophile
intranet

jihadist
kazillion
latte
mbaqanga
McJob
megaplex
microarray
minitower
multiculti
nanomachine
netiquette
netizen
olestra
perestroika
phytoplasma
piehole
pikeminnow
proteome

psychobabble
SARS
spam
spinmeister
statin
tatsoi
telomerase
thirtysomething
velociraptor
wakeboard
webcast
webmaster
yoctosecond
yottabyte
zeptosecond
zettabyte
zouk

The K's Have It

Look at the lists for each language and notice that there is something mentioned about the spelling of /k/ in almost every list. Correctly spelling the /k/ sound in English words is sometimes like flipping a coin. *If you must guess* how to spell the /k/ sound in a word that has a non–Western European language of origin, especially one that uses a non-Roman alphabet, *your safest guess is to spell it with a k.*

study lists. Look them up and note how many different language origins they represent:

Abyssinian	**Havarti**	**Tacitean**
Afrikaans	**Islamic**	**Tammanyism**
Ananias	**Jainism**	**Torquemada**
Bauhaus	**Krugerrand**	**Ulyssean**
Berber	**Latino**	**Unitarian**
Boyg	**Madagascar**	**Vatican**
Camelot	**Micawber**	**Vesuvian**
Charleston	**Nietzschean**	**Wednesday**
Cimmerian	**Nigerois**	**Wesak**
December	**Olympian**	**Yinglish**
Doppler	**Rankine**	**Zendo**
Euterpean	**Rastafarian**	**Zoroastrian**
Geronimo	**Sikkimese**	
Hadean	**Solomonic**	

Study Your Interests

What are your hobbies? Whether you like dogs, cats, or insects; collect coins, posters, or sneakers; enjoy music, sewing, or karate—you have a rich source of spelling bee words at your fingertips. People around the world enjoy many of the same activities, so the vocabulary that goes with your hobby may well be an international one. As you learn more about your hobby, make a note of good spelling words and look them up in the dictionary to find out more about where they came from. The very best hobby for a speller, though, may be learning foreign languages!

CHAPTER 5

A Few Rules and Many Exceptions

Spelling in English (and most other languages, for that matter) has two features that tend to drive many people crazy: rules and exceptions. (For our purposes, a rule is anything that constitutes a common English spelling pattern, and an exception is anything that doesn't seem to fit into a common English spelling pattern.)

Keep in mind as you study this chapter that some of the "rules" you may already have learned are really more like guidelines with many exceptions.

Don't Just Stand There— Ask!

In the National Spelling Bee and in most other spelling bees, when you are given a word you are allowed to ask about its part of speech. This piece of information can be valuable because some suffixes and word parts sound alike but are spelled differently and belong to different parts of speech, like *-us* and *-ous*. It's always wiser to make absolutely sure of your information than to rush boldly into a spelling that may not be correct.

Since many spellers flounder on the rocks of similar-sounding affixes or are not sure when the affix affects the spelling of the root word, this chapter is devoted to presenting prefix and suffix spelling rules and exceptions as clearly as possible. After some general rules comes a short section on troublesome prefixes, which are actually few in number. The rest of the chapter focuses on the far greater number of rules and exceptions that apply to suffixes, which determine a word's part of speech, and we've sorted them that way.

Keep in mind as you study this chapter that some of the "rules" you may already have learned—like "*i* before *e* except after *c,* or when sounded like *a* as in *neighbor* and *weigh*" are really more like guidelines with many exceptions. Keep your mind, eyes, and ears open for examples that confirm patterns you know, as well as exceptions that you should write down.

Some Very General Rules

Let's begin with the rules that apply across the board to words from every part of speech.

Drop the final *e* before a suffix beginning with a vowel, unless all the following three criteria are met: (1) the word ends in *-ge* or *-ce,* (2) the suffix begins with *a* or *o,* and (3) the "soft" sound of *g* or *c* is to be retained. Examples: *alleging, intoning; advantageous, noticeable.*

Double the final consonant before adding a suffix beginning with a vowel if the word has one syllable or an accent on the last syllable. If the accent shifts with the addition of the suffix, do not double the final consonant. Examples: *abetting, beginner, rappelled; conference, reference.*

*A winner, a loser. Peg McCarthy of Topeka, Kansas, spells the word **deification** to win the 51st National Spelling Bee. Runner-up Lyn Sue Kahng from San Diego, California, hangs her head in defeat.*

Future Fed Head Eliminated with "Edelweiss"

Ben S. Bernanke, the chairman of the Federal Reserve Board and the nation's most visible economist, was once an eleven-year-old speller representing South Carolina at the National Spelling Bee. Unfortunately, Dr. Bernanke misspelled **edelweiss** and does not get to add the National Spelling Bee championship to his list of accomplishments.

Rule 3: Changing *y* to *i*

Words that end in *y* usually change the *y* to *i* before a suffix, unless the *y* is the second of two vowels at the end of the word or the suffix begins with *i*. Examples: *happiness, silliest; grayness, boyish, flying.*

Rule 4: Adding a Prefix

Whenever a prefix is added to a word, the spelling of the word itself remains the same. Examples: *mis- + shapen = misshapen; im- + mutable = immutable.* This is one of the simplest rules to follow because it has no exceptions!

Rule 5: *i* before *e*

It may be what we call a "chestnut," but the *i*-before-*e* spelling rule really does work most of the time. In this two-vowel combination (linguists call it a *digraph* when the two letters make a single sound), put the *i* first unless the combination immediately follows a *c*, or has a long *a* sound. Examples: *believe; perceive, ceiling; vein, feint.* If the two vowels are pronounced separately, as in *science, concierge,* and *deity,* they should be spelled as pronounced rather than according to the rule. This rule also does not include nouns ending in *cy* that form a plural by changing *y* to *i* and adding *es*, like *vacancy/vacancies.*

Most of the remaining common exceptions are:

caffeine	**plebeian**
codeine	**protein**
counterfeit	**reveille**

either
feisty
foreign
forfeit
heifer
height
heir
heist
kaleidoscope
leisure
neither

seismic
seize
sleight
sovereign
stein
surfeit
their
veil
weir
weird

Keep your eyes peeled for other exceptions as you study!

A Few Pesky Prefixes

Most prefixes and combining forms have a distinct sound, but that won't help you if you just haven't studied *gnath-* and therefore don't know about the silent *g*. Merriam-Webster's *Dictionary of Prefixes, Suffixes, and Combining Forms,* available on the Scripps National Spelling Bee site (www.spellingbee.com), is your best bet for learning as many as you can. To give you a head start, we've pulled out a few common prefixes and combining forms that sound alike when placed at the front of a word,

ante
apparatus
aquacade
axel
badminton
bisque
cribbage
croupier
deuce
dreidel
gambit
glissade
heptathlon
hoyle
jackknife
marathon
mogul
mulligan
palooka
pelota
pentathlon
regatta
schuss
scrimmage
skijoring
slalom
snorkeling
telemark
tournament
trampolining
velodrome

Creature Feature

D o you like weird monster movies—the ones with English dialogue dubbed in? Words for interesting creatures come from many different languages. Here are just a few—some familiar, others probably new to you.

Frankenstein
harpy
hircocervus
kraken
makara
marmennill
nix
onocentaur
orc
Sasquatch
snallygaster
sphinx
triton
whangdoodle

anti- and ante-

Ante- is a Latin prefix meaning "before" or "prior." *Anti-* is also Latin but means "against."

antebellum	**anticyclone**
antenatal	**antifreeze**
antescript	**antigravity**

cyno- and Sino-

Cyno- means "dog" and *Sino-* (which is usually capitalized, as in *Sinogram*) means "Chinese." The word *cynosure,* "a center of attention or interest," came from Latin and Greek roots that originally meant "a dog's tail."

dis- and dys-

Dys- means "abnormal," "diseased," "difficult," "faulty," "impaired," "bad," or "unfavorable," and often comes at the beginning of scientific or medical terms. *Dis-* means "opposite of," "contrary of," "absence of," "not," or "completely." Confusingly, it can also sometimes mean "dys-," so it's worth looking up the words that start with *dys-* in the dictionary.

dysentery	**disadvantage**
dyslexia	**disagree**
dyspeptic	**disheveled**

em-, en-, im-, and in-

These are not really homophones, but do sound somewhat alike. Be careful when spelling them aloud in competition. *Em-/en-* means "put into or on to," "cause to be," "provide with," or "thoroughly" (often in verbs whose meaning is not

very different without the prefix, as *tangle/entangle).* *Em-* is used before *b, m,* or *p* and *en-* is used in all other circumstances: *embrace, enable, enslave.* *Im-/in-* also follows that rule (and adds two more: *il-* is used before *l* and *ir-* is used before *r*). It means "not" *(immutable, imprudent)* or "in," "inward," "toward," "on" *(inculcate, impound).*

Any word having to do with flowers or blooming plants may contain the combining form *flori-,* as in *floriculture* and *florisugent. Fluor-/fluoro-* refers to the element fluorine—which is not a fragrant substance at all, but a poisonous gas at room temperature! *Fluorescent* light bulbs contain hydrogen fluoride, which gives them a cool glow. Something that is *florescent* is blooming or flourishing.

Peri- means "surrounding," "around," or "near," and is often used in scientific words like *perihelion, periocular,* and *periodontal. Par-/para-* means "beside" (as in *paramedic,* who works in cooperation with a doctor), "beyond," "faulty or abnormal," and also has two scientific meanings ("derived from an original sediment," used in geological terms, and "isomeric or polymeric

The Prepared Mind

" **I**n my opinion, it's impossible to be over-prepared. I remember a common saying from the national finals: 'I knew every word except the one I got!' But with respect to competition advice, chance favors the prepared mind. Greek and Latin roots are invaluable, but the prepared speller also knows the words that do not conform and knows when to break the rules. I made a compendium of words I hadn't heard of from several different library books, then confirmed each one in *Webster's Third New International.* It was a very tedious process, but there's a lot of serendipity in the process. "

—GEORGE THAMPY,
2000 National
Spelling Bee champion
(winning word: demarche)

I Could Spell That in My Sleep

"My mom and sister used to drill me for hours in the weeks before the state and national competition. My sister, Anne, and I rode a bus up to the ski slopes. She would drill me the whole way up and back. My mom would drill me all the way until bedtime. More than once, family members caught me spelling in my sleep."

—KATIE KERWIN McCRIMMON, *1979 National Spelling Bee champion (winning word: maculature)*

with," used in chemistry). Its meaning is a little hard to trace in the many words that contain it, like *paragon, parasite,* and *paraphrase,* so try to learn as many *peri-* and *para-* words as you can. If you do nothing else, at least learn the difference between *parameter* and *perimeter*—two words that are often confused.

techno- and tekno-

Words with the combining form *techno-* are very common and have to do with the application of knowledge to practical matters. There are only two English words that use *tekno-,* which comes from the Greek *teknon,* meaning "child": *teknonymy* and *teknonymous,* both referring to the naming of children for their parents.

Verbs

Standard verb endings are *-s, -es, -ing,* and *-ed.* For the most part, verb inflections (how you change the ending of the verb to match the subject and tense of the sentence) follow the general rules above. There are a few additional rules:

Rule: If the verb ends in *s, z, x, sh,* or *ch,* add *-es* to form the third person present: *caress/caresses, fizz/fizzes, coax/coaxes, crash/crashes, march/marches.*

Rule: If the verb ends in a single vowel *y*, change it to *i* before adding *-es* for third person present or *-ed* for past tense: *marry/marries/married, beautify/beautifies/beautified.* Do not change the *y* before the present participle ending *-ing: beautifying.* If the verb has a vowel before the *y*, treat it as you would a consonant ending: *annoy/annoys/annoyed, survey/surveys/surveyed.*

Rule: If the verb ends in *c*, add a *k* before *-ed* or *-ing* (*bivouac/bivouacked/bivouacking, panic/panicked/panicking, picnic/picnicked/picnicking, traffic/trafficked/trafficking*).

Rule: For one-syllable verbs ending in *ye* or *oe*, keep the final *e* before *-ing*, but drop it before *-ed*. Examples: *eye/eyeing/eyed, shoe/shoeing/shoed.*

Rule: If the verb ends in *ie* or *ee*, drop the final *e* before *-ed: belie/belied, free/freed.* If the verb ends in *ie*, change it to *y* before adding *-ing: tying, vying.*

Last In, First Out

When you are given an unfamiliar word that originated in one language but went through another language or languages, use spelling guidelines from the most recent language—i.e., the one it went through just before coming into English.

"*Be thankful that in English a noun's form stays the same no matter what its role in a sentence.***"**

There are three words that end in *z* preceded by a vowel in which the *z* is doubled before adding -es: *quiz/quizzes, spaz/spazzes, whiz/whizzes.*

The Sad and Lonely Q

There are just a very few words in English that use Q without its friend U:

faqih
Inupiaq
nastaliq
Qatari
qintar
qiviut
qiyas
taqlid
zindiq

-ise, -ize, or -yze?

Most verbs that end in the "eyes" sound have Latin roots and are spelled *-ize*. Those that are spelled *-ise* generally (though not always) come from Old French or Middle French. There aren't very many of them. If you don't see a few you expect (like *surprise*) on this list, it's because they can be spelled either *-ise* or *-ize*.

abscise	improvise
advise	incise
chastise	previse
compromise	reprise
demise	revise
despise	rise
devise	surmise
disguise	televise
exercise	vise
franchise	wise

The Latin noun combining form *-lysis* has led to the verb combining form *-lyze,* which means "to produce or undergo disintegration or dissolution" and is used in the following verbs (and similar verbs with prefixes, like *psycho-analyze* and *electrodialyze*):

acetolyze	electrolyze
ammonolyze	hemolyze
analyze	hydrolyze

autolyze	**paralyze**
catalyze	**pyrolyze**
cytolyze	**solvolyze**
dialyze	

So if you hear an *l* before the "eyes" sound, first check to see if it is a variant of one of these verbs; if it is not, go ahead and spell it *-lize*.

Nouns

Nouns are the building blocks of a language, the first words most of us learn. Many nouns came directly into English from another language; others were made by modifying another noun *(neighborhood = neighbor + -hood)* or a verb *(aspirant = aspir(e) + -ant)*. Luckily for us, the form of a noun stays the same in English, no matter what function it plays in the sentence. Many folks in the world aren't so lucky.

Plural Nouns

There are rules for forming plural nouns and many exceptions to the rules. Some of these arise when a word has hung on desperately to a historical plural that belongs to the language it came from or to an older form of English.

Regular English plurals are formed by adding *-s* to the singular: *lemur/lemurs*. If the singular noun ends in *s, x, z, ch,* or *sh,* the

aioli
avgolemono
beignet
bouillon
cannoli
choucroute
chipolata
espagnole
focaccia
fricassee
jambalaya
kaiseki
lyonnaise
madrilene
mamaliga
milchig
mostaccioli
moussaka
paella
pansit
persillade
raclette
rotisserie
roux
sarsaparilla
schnecke
tagliarini
tandoori
tempeh
tiramisu
vichyssoise
vindaloo
yosenabe

No Blurting!

"Words suddenly seem much harder and more confusing when you receive them onstage at a bee than at home from your mom! I would encourage spellers to try to stay completely focused on the pronouncer and the word and to block out all other distractions. Take your time with an unfamiliar word to explore all possible spellings and resist the temptation to blurt out your first instinct!"

—PEG MCCARTHY,
*1978 National Spelling
Bee champion*

ending *-es* is added to form the plural: *quartz/ quartzes.* This adds a syllable to the pronunciation and makes it actually possible to pronounce the plural! There are three words that end in *z* preceded by a vowel in which the *z* is doubled before adding *-es: quiz/quizzes, spaz/spazzes, whiz/whizzes.*

If the noun ends in a vowel or *l* plus *f,* we usually change the *f* to a *v* and add *-es: loaf/ loaves, thief/thieves, calf/calves, shelf/shelves.* There are some exceptions, including *aperitifs, beliefs, chefs, chiefs, clefs, massifs, motifs, proofs.* Both forms exist for some words: *handkerchieves/handkerchiefs, rooves/roofs, scarves/scarfs.* Note: This change is also made for a few nouns that have a silent *e* after the *f: knife/knives, life/lives, wife/wives.*

If the singular noun is a common noun (i.e., not a name) and ends in a single vowel *y,* the plural is formed by changing the *y* to *ie* and adding *-s: blueberry, blueberries.* If *y* is the second of two vowels, we keep it and add *-s: boys, monkeys.* If it is a name, we just add *-s* to form a plural: *Avery, Averys.* Note that this is properly used when speaking of more than one person in the same family: *The Averys have moved in next door.* (Never use an apostrophe to form

a plural noun! The right time to use an apostrophe is when forming a possessive or a contraction. The possessive form of *Avery* is *Avery's,* and the possessive form of the plural is *Averys': Lauren Avery's poodle will sit up and shake hands with red-haired girls. People say the Averys' broom closet is haunted.* Adding the apostrophe and *-s* effectively turns the noun into an adjective because it gives information about the noun that follows it. In a contraction, the apostrophe stands in for a missing letter: *Susan's* [Susan is] *going to Hawaii next week with her grandparents. They're* [They are] *planning to go surfing.*

Some nouns of Latin origin have kept the Latin form in the plural. Latin nouns that end in *a* typically add *-e* to form the plural:

alumna	alumnae
stria	striae
regina	reginae
petechia	petechiae
medusa	medusae
vertebra	vertebrae

Latin nouns that end in *us* usually form the plural by removing the *us* and adding *-i:*

alumnus	alumni
oculus	oculi
torus	tori
cubitus	cubiti
cumulus	cumuli
euripus	euripi
magus	magi
stimulus	stimuli

Sammy Totino of Chesterland, Ohio, misspells the word **ocarina** *during the 74th Annual National Spelling Bee.*

Woof, Woof!

Some words, called **onomatopoeia**, originated as an imitation of natural sounds—in fact, some linguists have developed a theory (sometimes known as the "bow-wow theory") that this is how all spoken language began. There are onomatopoeia in every language.

Latin nouns that end in *-um* or *-on* often replace that ending with *-a* to form the plural:

addendum	**addenda**
bacterium	**bacteria**
curriculum	**curricula**
datum	**data**
criterion	**criteria**
noumenon	**noumena**
phenomenon	**phenomena**

Latin- and Greek-based nouns that end in *-sis* usually form the plural just by changing the *i* to an *e*:

analysis	**analyses**
basis	**bases**
catharsis	**catharses**
crisis	**crises**
ellipsis	**ellipses**
emphasis	**emphases**
exegesis	**exegeses**
genesis	**geneses**
paralysis	**paralyses**
parenthesis	**parentheses**
synthesis	**syntheses**
synopsis	**synopses**

Other nouns of Latin origin have taken on the regular English plural forms *-s* and *-es* exclusively, like *dementia/dementias, echidna/echidnas, trapezius/trapeziuses, tinnitus/tinnituses, exodus/exoduses.* Still others offer the choice of forming their plurals in either the Latin or English way, as shown in this table:

SINGULAR	LATIN PLURAL	ENGLISH PLURAL
alga	algae	algas
formula	formulae	formulas
nebula	nebulae	nebulas
nova	novae	novas
patina	patinae	patinas
persona	personae	personas
scapula	scapulae	scapulas
cactus	cacti	cactuses
fungus	fungi	funguses
nimbus	nimbi	nimbuses
nucleus	nuclei	nucleuses
octopus	octopi	octopuses
opus	opera	opuses
radius	radii	radiuses
thymus	thymi	thymuses
crisis	crises	crisises
eclipsis	eclipses	eclipsises
cerebellum	cerebella	cerebellums
plectrum	plectra	plectrums
podium	podia	podiums

Good to Goal

"I can vividly remember being a young elementary school student and imagining myself winning the National Spelling Bee. I even had dreams of winning long before I did. Achieving that goal took a tremendous amount of work, along with great luck. But it taught me the value of envisioning success. Many times since the bee, I have set goals and achieved them. I learned how fun it was to win awards and reap the rewards."

—KATIE KERWIN MCCRIMMON, *1979 National Spelling Bee champion*

A small number of nouns from Latin end in *-ix* or *-ex,* and these sometimes form the plural by changing *x* to *-ces: genetrix/genetrices.* Others use the regular English formation and add *-es* to the word: *crucifix/crucifixes.* Most of the *-ix* nouns, however, offer a choice: *appendix/appendices/appendixes, matrix/matrices/matrixes.*

A few nouns from Latin maintain the same form of the word whether singular or plural: *series, species.* As with English nouns that form

the plural this way *(moose, sheep, aircraft),* there are not very many.

There are a few nouns of French origin ending in *-eau* that can form the plural by adding *-x* (which can either be silent or pronounced /z/): *bandeau/bandeaux, bureau/bureaux, eau/eaux,* for example. Some of these also offer the English plural form *-s: chapeau/chapeaux/chapeaus,* and some have

2004 *While National Spelling Bee champion David Scott Tidmarsh addressed his school, Edison Intermediate School in South Bend, Indiana, Edison students stood with cards spelling out his winning word,* **autochthonous.**

A few nouns from Latin maintain the same form of the word whether singular or plural, like *series* and *species*.

only the -*s* form: *jetteau/jetteaus, rideau/rideaus.* Confusingly, the -*s* ending is also pronounced /z/, so proceed cautiously when spelling one of these plurals.

Some nouns ending in *o* add *s* for the plural ending (*albedos, logos, pianos, solos*), and some (*echoes, heroes, potatoes, tomatoes, torpedoes*) add -*es*. Many accept either spelling: *pinto/pintos/pintoes, stucco/stuccos/stuccoes, volcano/volcanos/volcanoes.* If there is another vowel before the *o*, the ending is usually -*s:* *cameos, studios, duos.* Otherwise, there doesn't appear to be a pattern to nouns ending in *o*, so it's best to memorize as many of these plurals as you can.

There are other nouns in English, mostly those with a Middle English/Old English heritage, that have irregular plurals, like *child/ children, goose/geese, man/men, mouse/mice, ox/oxen, tooth/teeth, woman/women.* Others are plurals that have no unique singular: *cattle, police.* Fortunately, most of these are very common and quite easy to spell.

Some onomatopoeically-named birds talk about themselves all the time! Listen to the **bobwhite, cuckoo, curlew, dickcissel, kiwi, motmot, siskin, towhee, whippoor-will,** and **willet.**

Noun Suffixes

Suffixes that are unstressed and contain a schwa are often confusing because they could be spelled multiple ways. We'll address these first.

-er, -or, or -ar? To make a "person or thing that performs an action" noun from a verb, we

From Bee to Bar

"For me, spelling competition fostered valuable time management habits that I would later employ in high school, at Yale University, and at Columbia Law School. Moreover, spelling under hot lights, before flashing camera bulbs, and hundreds of spectators, conditioned me to maintain poise under pressure, whether in a round of interscholastic debate or in a mock trial courtroom."

—CRAIG BUCKI,
National Spelling Bee finalist, 1995 and 1996; law student

usually add -*er* or -*or*. Unfortunately, there aren't any hard-and-fast rules that govern which one is used, but there are some general guidelines. The suffix -*er* is Middle English/Old English, and -*or* is its Latin cousin. Often, if the verb that forms the noun comes from Middle English, we use -*er*. These are what we usually think of as our simple "doer" nouns: *farmer, greeter, hunter, invader, miner.* If the verb in question has a Latin root, we often add -*or* to form the noun: *director, incubator, moderator, perpetrator, sculptor, separator.* Note that in both cases, any silent *e* at the end of the verb is dropped, as it is before any suffix beginning with a vowel.

For nouns that are not formed from verbs, the "ur" ending is somewhat more likely to be spelled -*er* as in *barber, milliner,* and *monster.* It's worth memorizing some common exceptions like *doctor, gladiator, mentor,* and *sector.*

The suffix -*er* is also used in adjectives to show a comparative degree, as in *fleecier* and *brasher.* The adjectival ending -*ar,* which means "of or belonging to," "resembling," or "being" (as in *molecular, triangular,* and *vascular*), is also easy to confuse with -*er* and -*or.*

These are two of the reasons why it's impor-tant to know whether you're spelling an adjective

For nouns made from Middle English/Old English verbs use -er; use -or for nouns formed from a Latin verb.

or a noun! Also, there are some nouns ending in *-ar* that are spelled the same way as the adjective that describes them, such as *tubercular,* which is both an adjective meaning "relating to or affected by tuberculosis" and a noun meaning "a person having tuberculosis."

There are a few other common nouns that end in *-ar,* and you should make a point of memorizing them. Some are compound words formed from the one-syllable nouns *bar, car, star,* and *war.* Others are:

agar	circular
alegar	collar
altar	commissar
antimacassar	dollar
beggar	feldspar
burglar	liar
calendar	poplar
caterpillar	scholar
cedar	sugar
cheddar	tartar
cigar	vicar
cinnabar	vinegar

-ant or -ent, -ance or -ence? The suffixes *-ant* and *-ent* can be used to create nouns and adjectives, and they sound alike when pronounced. The suffixes *-ance* and *-ence* can be used to create nouns. They, too, sound alike when pronounced.

*Rebecca Sealfon of Brooklyn, New York, wins the 70th Annual National Spelling Bee. Sealfon overcame a bad case of nerves and 244 other contestants to win the bee by correctly spelling the word **euonym**.*

A Few Spicy Words

The terms for many popular Mexican foods, like **tamale** and **chipotle,** and even some foods that we don't necessarily think of as Mexican, like **avocado** and **chocolate,** come from Nahuatl, the language spoken by the Aztecs when the Spanish explorer Hernán Cortés arrived in 1519.

There is no rule that can help you with most of the words that have these endings. What can you say about the formation of *fragrant/fragrance* vs. *eminent/eminence,* for example? *Resistant/resistance* vs. *persistent/persistence*? Memorizing the spelling of words with these endings seems to be the best solution.

The following rules help out with a very small number of the words that have these endings. Try to remember these rules, and one of them just might be applicable when you must decide whether to use an *a* or an *e* to spell a word that calls for *-ant/-ance* or *-ent/-ence* as its final syllable.

Rule: After a soft *c* or a soft *g,* use *-ent/-ence.* After a hard *c* or a hard *g,* use *-ant/-ance.* (Note: Few words have a hard *c* or a hard *g* near the end.)

Examples:

Words with soft c *or* g *near the end:*

candescent/candescence
convergent/convergence
dehiscent/dehiscence
diligent/diligence
florescent/florescence
fluorescent/fluorescence
indulgent/indulgence
innocent/innocence
intelligent/intelligence
magnificent/magnificence
negligent/negligence
quiescent/quiescence

renascent/renascence

resurgent/resurgence

reticent/reticence

rubescent/rubescence

senescent/senescence

submergent/submergence

tumescent/tumescence

Words with hard c *or* g *near the end:*

elegant/elegance

extravagant/extravagance

mitigant/mitigance

significant/significance

Rule: If the verb form of the word ends in *-fer* and is accented on the final syllable, then the suffix will be *-ent* or *-ence.* With these words, if the suffix used is *-ent,* the addition of the suffix *-ial* is usually required to make the word complete.

Examples:

Verb form	*+ ent*	*+ ence*
defer	**deferential**	**deference**
infer	**inferential**	**inference**
prefer	**preferential**	**preference**
refer	**referential**	**reference**

beriberi
buccinator
calcaneus
carotid
catarrh
cerebellum
chiropody
dysplasia
edentulous
exeresis
exophasia
fibromyalgia
heterochromia
hyoid
hypersplenism
hypostasis
hypothalamus
maxillary
mecometer
mesomorph
metatarsal
nyctalopia
Paracelsian
paranephric
phlebotomy
phthisis
sarcology
somatotype
strabismus
sudoriferous
trichotillomania
trochlea
typhlology

Any Alternate Pronunciations?

Asking for alternate pronunciations of nouns ending with the "us" sound can sometimes be a huge help. If the ending of the noun is pronounced with only a regular schwa, the ending is often -*us*. Examples include **circus** and **hocus-pocus**. (Make a list of exceptions such as **fracas**.)

If the pronunciation of the ending of the noun is indicated with a dotted schwa, there will be at least two pronunciations: one with schwa and one with more of a short *i* sound. These words will often end in either -*ice* or -*ace*. Examples include **notice** and **populace**. (Make a list of exceptions such as **tennis**). But keep in mind that some words ending with a dotted schwa can have yet another pronunciation, one that can give away that pesky vowel indicated by the dotted schwa. For example, the endings of the following words can be

(continued on next page)

Rule: If the verb form of the word has an *a* in the final syllable, then the suffix will be -*ant* or -*ance*.

Examples:

Verb form	+ ant	+ ance
defoliate	**defoliant**	
delegate	**delegant**	
deviate	**deviant**	**deviance**
dominate	**dominant**	**dominance**
evacuate	**evacuant**	
hesitate	**hesitant**	**hesitance**
radiate	**radiant**	**radiance**
react	**reactant**	**reactance**
resonate	**resonant**	**resonance**
tolerate	**tolerant**	**tolerance**

Remember to add these and similar words to your lists or spelling notebook as you run across them in your studying. Word familiarity will likely be the biggest help to you when you have to decide whether to use -*ant*/-*ance* or -*ent*/-*ence*.

-*us*, -*ice*, or -*ace*? Nouns ending in the "us" sound are almost always spelled with the ending -*us*, like *abacus, cubitus, cumulus, hiatus, nexus, tetanus.* However, there are a number of nouns whose pronunciation ends in a sound very close to "us" that have the spelling -*ice* (like *accomplice, armistice, avarice, bodice, chalice, hospice, lattice, malefice, office, orifice, pumice*) or -*ace* (like *boniface, bullace, furnace, grimace, solace, surface, terrace*). The difference in the phoneme is that the schwa is dotted, giving a vowel a sound a little closer to a short *i*.

Word familiarity will be your best friend when you have to decide whether to use -*ant* or -*ent*.

Look up some of these words and practice this subtle difference in pronunciation. This has tripped up many spellers in spelling bees around the country, as well as at the national finals! And remember: When you hear the "us" sound at the end of a word, it is extremely important to determine whether you are being asked to spell a noun or an adjective.

(continued from previous page)

pronounced with either a schwa, a short *i* associated with the dotted schwa, or the gift of a long a: **grimace** and **boniface.** Bottom line: Ask for all of the pronunciations!

Adjectives

Most adjective endings in English are fairly straightforward to spell and not easily confused, such as -*al, -ic, -ive,* and -*less.* A small number of them, however, cause a large number of misses in spelling bees. Here are a few tips to help you when the going gets rough:

-*ful* Even though -*ful* does mean "full of," it is always spelled with one *l* when you attach it to a word: *guileful, respectful.*

-*able* or -*ible*?

- Say the word minus the suffix out loud. If an actual English word remains, the

Remember that there are about five times as many words that end in *-able* as in *-ible*.

suffix is more likely to be spelled *-able: accept/acceptable, inhabit/inhabitable, respect/respectable, work/workable.* This is usually, but not always, true, so memorize some of the most common exceptions:

combustible	**exhaustible**
contemptible	**flexible**
convertible	**forcible**
corruptible	**responsible**
deductible	**sensible**
digestible	**suggestible**

- If the root is an English word ending in *e,* drop the *e* before adding *-able,* unless the consonant before the *e* is *g* or *c: perceive/perceivable, excite/excitable, embrace/embraceable, change/changeable.* If the ending is *-ible,* always drop the *e*

The sound you don't want to hear.

ending in the root: *forcible, responsible.*

- Words that are not formed directly from an unchanged English word are more likely to have the *-ible* ending: *divisible, fungible, irascible.*

- If the root ends in a long *i* sound, the suffix will be *-able: friable, viable.*

- There are a number of words that can be spelled with either ending, like *condensable/condensible, ignitable/ ignitible, possessable/possessible.* Be aware of these, but don't spend a lot of time worrying about them.

- Finally, if you really have no clue whether to use the *-able* or *-ible* ending, just remember that there are about five times as many words that end in *-able* as in *-ible.* In fact, it's a good idea to memorize at least the most common *-ible* words, because there aren't that many of them. Some good ones to know are:

audible	**intelligible**
compatible	**legible**
credible	**negligible**
edible	**permissible**
eligible	**plausible**
fallible	**possible**
feasible	**reprehensible**
gullible	**susceptible**
horrible	**terrible**
incorrigible	**transmissible**
indelible	**visible**

Bar-Bee-Q

"Number one: Work hard. Winning will not come without work and effort put into it. Number two: Have fun. I didn't participate in the spelling bee because I hated it. I loved the adrenaline rush I got at the microphone. I loved the National Spelling Bee because there were so many fun things I could do—the barbecue, tours, or just socializing with my friends. It was a wonderful experience— one to last a lifetime. So ENJOY IT!"

—ANURAG KASHYAP,
*2005 National
Spelling Bee champion*
(winning word:
appoggiatura)

KISS

" **A**t the bee, keep it simple for success! If you have to spell a word you don't remember seeing before, always remember that words are, by and large, spelled the way they sound. At home, remember that the most important thing you will win from studying for a spelling bee is knowledge, not prizes or fame."

—JACQUES BAILLY, *1980 National Spelling Bee champion and current Scripps National Spelling Bee pronouncer*

-eous or -ious? Most of the words that end in *-eous* and *-ious* come from Latin, and the Latin roots tend to determine what the ending will be. Without going too far into Latin spelling rules, we can make some simple generalizations:

- Adjectives related to material composition or to sciences like biology, chemistry, and geology usually end in *-eous: cutaneous, herbaceous, osseous, vitreous.*

- Words related to taxonomic matters like phylum, class, order, family, genus, or species often have the ending *-aceous: liliaceous, pomaceous.*

- Adjectives related to human feelings, qualities, or actions usually end in *-ious: harmonious, laborious, malicious, suspicious.* There are some obvious exceptions, *courteous, erroneous, righteous,* and *spontaneous* are among them.

- If you can think of a related word ending in *-ion,* the correct ending is usually *-ious: ambition/ambitious, caution/cautious, infection/infectious, rebellion/rebellious, religion/religious.*

-cious or -tious? There are approximately equal numbers of words with these endings in *Webster's Third,* but when you remove the entries that are obsolete or have alternate spellings, *-cious* has the edge. If you know whether the noun that is the basis of the word ends in *-cion* or *-tion,* you're in business when it comes to forming the adjective. Here are some of the most common *-cious* and *-tious* adjectives:

-cious vs. *-tious*

audacious	judicious	salacious	fictitious
atrocious	loquacious	spacious	flirtatious
auspicious	lubricious	specious	fractious
autoecious	luscious	stenecious	infectious
avaricious	malicious	suspicious	licentious
bibacious	mendacious	tenacious	nutritious
bodacious	meretricious	velocious	obreptitious
capacious	minacious	veracious	oppositious
capricious	mordacious	vicious	ostentatious
conscious	nugacious	vivacious	pretentious
contumacious	officious	voracious	propitious
delicious	pernicious	....	rambunctious
edacious	perspicacious	adventitious	repetitious
efficacious	pertinacious	ambitious	scrumptious
fallacious	pervicacious	bumptious	seditious
feracious	precious	captious	stillatitious
ferocious	precocious	cautious	superstitious
fugacious	prejudicious	circumlocutious	suppositious
gracious	procacious	conscientious	surreptitious
hellacious	pugnacious	contentious	tendentious
heteroecious	rapacious	expeditious	tralatitious
homoecious	sagacious	factitious	vexatious

-us or -ous? The schwa-plus-*s*, or "us" sound, at the end of many adjectives is *almost* always spelled *-ous: membranous, scrupulous, vainglorious, vociferous.* Some exceptions to this rule are words such as *Columbus, Damascus, Mauritius*—adjectives that mean "of or from" a particular place, where the place name happens to end in *-us.* Others are Latin adjectives that have retained the Latin form *-us,* often because they are part of a scientific or academic vocabulary that has historically leaned heavily on

Rhonda Jones of Harmony, North Carolina, anxiously waits to be called for the 50th Annual National Spelling Bee.

Commonly Misspelled Words

Listed below are some of the most commonly misspelled non-homonymic English words. Getting them right in life—on school papers, college applications, and resumes—will mark you as detail oriented, literate, and smart. Make a list of them in your spelling notebook and add to it when you find other everyday misspellings. Look online for lists of other commonly misspelled words and ask your teachers what some of their favorites are.

accidentally	disappear	lieutenant	recommend
accommodate	disappoint	marshmallow	refrigerator
accordion	dissipate	millennium	renown
accumulate	drunkenness	miniature	rhythm
acquaintance	dumbbell	miscellaneous	ridiculous
acquire	ecstasy	mischief	sacrilegious
acquit	embarrass	mischievous	sandal
amateur	exercise	misogyny	savvy
believe	exhilarate	missile	seize
breath	existence	misspell	sensible
breathe	Fahrenheit	necessary	separate
broccoli	fiery	occasion	sergeant
calendar	grammar	occurrence	sheriff
camouflage	guttural	odyssey	siege
Caribbean	handkerchief	parallel	similar
cartilage	harass	parliament	sorcerer
cemetery	height	pastime	subpoena
commemorate	hypocrisy	pharaoh	tariff
congratulations	immediately	playwright	threshold
consensus	inadvertent	poinsettia	tongue
Dalmatian	incidentally	prejudice	tragedy
defendant	incredible	presumptuous	tyranny
definite	independent	privilege	until
desiccate	infinite	pronunciation	vacuum
desperate	inoculate	pursue	vicious
deterrence	irresistible	raspberry	weird
dilemma	lavender	receipt	
diorama	liaison	receive	

Homonyms:
Be Discreet, Not Discrete

Many homonyms (words that sound alike but have different meanings and often different spellings) and near homonyms (like *conscience / conscious*) seem to be misspelled more often than not! This is by no means a complete list of homonyms, but the ones shown here are some of the most common and therefore the most commonly misspelled. Some of them are not generally used in spelling bees because they are contractions and have an apostrophe, but they are included here because they are very important to know. As a good speller, you should make a special point of using common homonyms correctly.

accept	boarder	die	metal	pedal
except	border	dye	mettle	peddle
ad	brake	discreet	morning	principal
add	break	discrete	mourning	principle
affect	cellar	eminent	muscle	role
effect	seller	imminent	mussel	roll
allowed	cereal	immanent	naval	stationary
aloud	serial	forth	navel	stationery
altar	climb	fourth	overdo	than
alter	clime	hear	overdue	then
band	coarse	here	palate	their
banned	course	heroin	pallet	there
bare	complement	heroine	palette	they're
bear	compliment	it's	passed	threw
basis	conscience	its	past	through
bases	conscious	lightening	peace	who's
basses	currant	lightning	piece	whose
bridal	current	loose	peak	yore
bridle	desert	lose	peek	you're
	dessert	medal	pique	your
		meddle		

Just add *-ly* to the adjective to make the adverb.

Latin: *anticus, camus, castellatus, emeritus, intermedius, mammatus, maximus, minimus, omnibus, pararectus, redivivus, solus.* There are a very few other exceptions like *antivirus, bogus, Celsius,* and *interstimulus.*

See the discussion of *-ace, -ice,* and *-us* in the nouns sidebar on page 112 for further related information.

Adverbs

ost adverbs end in *-ly.* A few that do not have retained an adverb ending from another language, like the following:

-im (literatim, passim, seriatim, verbatim)
-ad (aborad, anteriad, frontad, mediad, palmad)

(these are typically musical terms)
-issimo (dolcissimo, fortissimo, pianissimo)
-mente (furiosamente, rapidamente, soavemente)

There are also several adverb endings that come from Middle English: *-ward/-wards, -ways,* and *-wise: southward, throneward, sternways, clockwise, lengthwise.* They are almost always applied to root words that also come from Middle English, and so the resulting words are usually very easy to spell.

N ote that *politicly* and *politically* have different meanings! *Politicly* is formed from *politic,* and it means "craftily" or "shrewdly." *Politically,* which is formed from *political,* means "from a point of view related to politics."

Duly Noted

I n a handful of adverbs, a final letter is dropped before adding *-ly*. These are **duly, illy,** and **truly.**

-ly or -ally? The confusion around these two adverb endings is easily eliminated by using a very simple rule: Just add *-ly* to the adjective to make the adverb! If the related adjective ends in *-al*, the adverb form will end in *-ally: accidental/accidentally, musical/musically, nominal/nominally, operational/operationally, social/socially.* Where the root adjective ends in *c*, an optional *-al* adjective ending has historically been applied before adding *-ly: fantastic/fantastically, symbolic/symbolically.* However, in all but a few of these words, the endings *-ally* and *-ly* are both permissible. The exceptions are *anticly, fantastically, politically, politicly,* and *romantically.*

CHAPTER 6

A ll spelling bees are fun and exciting, but the buzz and excitement at a National Spelling Bee are unique. Everyone knows that the spellers onstage are the very best out of the ten million hopeful spellers who started out at the classroom level not very many months before. And in only two days, those onstage spellers will wrestle with six hundred or so mind-bendingly difficult words, and one champion will emerge.

The first thing people usually notice at the National Spelling Bee finals is how big the stage is. It has to be because there will be more than 135 spellers sitting on it at the beginning of Round Two! The second round, which is the first oral round, is completed in two parts for exactly that reason: There are always too many contestants to put them all onstage at once.

"Are we ready at the records desk? Are the tapes rolling and recording? Are you ready, Dr. Bailly? Speller number one, Laura Ann Brown, representing the Birmingham Post-Herald of Birmingham, Alabama, you may approach the microphone."

The spellers onstage are seated in numerical order. Each speller wears his or her number on a placard, which also shows the city and state of the sponsoring newspaper. Numbers are assigned alphabetically, according to the name of the state and city. Sometimes there are late entries, in which case the new contestants are usually added to the end of the numerical list.

At the end of each round, staffers print out the round results and take them to the press desk for distribution to the public and to news media.

The microphone is center stage. The records desk is near the stage, in front of the audience. On it are several computers where National Spelling Bee staff members record how the contestants spell their words. The large media screens at the front of the auditorium are controlled from the records desk. Usually, one screen shows a running list of the words as they are spelled, and the other shows a photograph and brief bio of the speller at the microphone. At the end of each round, staffers print out the round results and take them to the press desk for distribution to the public and the news media.

Also near the stage is a podium for the pronouncer and assistant pronouncer, allowing the speller at the microphone to see their faces clearly (and vice versa). The judges' desk is directly in front of the microphone, ensuring a clear view of the speller. Occasionally, other Scripps National Spelling Bee officials sit at this desk as well.

There are two platforms at the rear of the auditorium, one for television equipment and

Folks back home can also get a copy of the round results. All they need to do is log on to www.spellingbee.com during the competition and click on Round Results.

Results are posted in real time, so curious minds don't have to wait until the end of a round to find out how their favorite spellers are faring. If access to the television broadcast is not an option, following along on the Web is the next best thing to being there!

The process of arriving at a finished word list begins nearly one year before.

Repetition is the Key. Repetition is the Key. Repetition . . .

"Heel, toe, heel, toe, slide, slide, slide, slide. . . ."

If you've ever done any line dancing, you're familiar with those words of the caller. If your memory is any good, it's not too long before you're saying the commands to yourself and no longer need the caller's prompt.

Some spellers learn new words in a similar way—repetition. They write a new word ten or so times, usually in a vertical line. This repetition seems to stamp the pattern of the word in the brain. Writing the word over and over sends a cadence to the brain that enables the speller to correctly spell the word.

the other for the National Spelling Bee's sound recording equipment. If there is an appeal of the judges' decision to eliminate a speller, it can be played directly into the judges' headphones or, in rare cases, into the room's sound system so that the entire audience can hear the replay.

How the Words Are Chosen

A three-member word panel chooses words for the Scripps National Spelling Bee from the current *Webster's Third New International Dictionary*. A typical list contains approximately one thousand words divided into sections: separate sections for each of the first ten or so rounds, another section for higher rounds, and a final section for Championship Words. The first round is a written test consisting of twenty-five items of increasing difficulty. All spellers take the same test.

The process of arriving at a finished list begins nearly one year before the list is used in competition. The panelists begin with a tentative list of words, often chosen from their everyday reading, news stories, and subjects of personal interest; other words are chosen directly from *Webster's Third*. The proposed words are checked against *Webster's Third* to make sure they are compatible with the official bee rules. If a proposed word is not listed in *Webster's Third*, it is removed from consideration. Word panelists DO NOT consult the *Consolidated Word List*—a nearly comprehensive list of words used in the Scripps National Spelling Bee since 1950—in choosing words for the new list.

Next, word panelists use information provided in *Webster's Third* to compose concise dictionary entries for their words. Each entry includes the word, its pronunciation, the part of speech, a definition, and a sentence illustrating the use of the word. Another bee official provides the language of origin information for each word, drawing heavily from information provided in *Webster's Third*.

Once the dictionary entries

Remember: The word panelists DO NOT consult the *Consolidated Word List* when selecting words for word lists. Spellers who happen to receive a word that is on the *Consolidated Word List* do so purely by coincidence. It's a good

"*If it's not in Webster's Third, it's not in the bee!***"**

guess that there has never been a round in national competition in which all the words in that round were on the *Consolidated Word List*. It's best to view the *Consolidated Word List* as a "study gift," *not* as a "study guide."

Members of the word panel meet in the autumn to review the rough draft.

For a Spelling Bee Word, No News Is Good News

A word's difficulty is often a sign of the times. If a word has recently been in the news quite a bit, the word's familiarity will cause it to receive a lower difficulty rating than it might otherwise receive, and will appear, if at all, earlier in the National Spelling Bee competition. For example, the word **cortege** experienced a big drop in difficulty in the year following Princess Diana's death because it had appeared in many news stories. In recent years, **cortege** has crept up in difficulty level because spellers have not had as many opportunities to encounter it.

are complete, the word list manager consolidates the information and produces a rough draft of the word list. Members of the word panel, along with some of the other bee officials, meet in the autumn to review the rough draft. This group revises many of the word entries and deletes some words from the list. During this meeting, each word is given a rating according to the panelists' and officials' best estimation of difficulty. When rating a word, consideration is given to the word's relative level of familiarity, the degree to which it can be spelled phonetically, and the degree to which the correct spelling may be deduced from knowledge of word roots and language patterns. A word's length in letters or number of syllables is sometimes a factor.

After the meeting, the word list manager edits the list again, reorders it according to the averaged ratings, and divides it into rounds. During another word panel meeting in the late winter before the national competition, the list is again discussed and some word placements are shifted if there is a consensus.

The final word list is sent to the pronouncer, who begins the process of researching each word's various pronunciations and compiling detailed notes on them. In May, the list is given to the judges for their review. Finally, one day before the competition begins, bee officials (pronouncers, judges, word panelists, word list manager, and the director) meet to review the word list, air any last-minute concerns, and make deletions, if needed.

After this lengthy process, which has incorporated many different meetings and levels of review, the list is deemed ready for use in competition.

The Written Round

The written, multiple-choice Round One has been a part of the national finals since 2002. It was adopted primarily because of the bee's time constraints, but most spellers like it because it gives them a chance to really show their stuff. Before 2002, spellers who were eliminated early in the bee had spelled only one or two words, but now every speller gets to make choices for the twenty-five items on the written test, plus spell at least one more word; even the spellers whose written test score will prevent passing the threshold of elimination spell one word—orally—in Round Two.

Each item on the written test counts for one point. The passing threshold is determined after

aubade
bariolage
cantabile
cantillate
celestina
decrescendo
diapason
divertissement
embouchure
euterpean
farandole
feroce
fortississimo
gamelan
glockenspiel
guaracha
lacrimando
larghetto
maestoso
misterioso
Orphean
ossia
pedaliter
piacevole
ridotto
risoluto
schottische
sfogato
solmizate
tacet
tarogato
tiralee
vide
vorspiel

Special Circumstances

The Scripps National Spelling Bee accommodates spellers with physical challenges involving sight, hearing, speech, or movement. If you have any condition that might impede your performance in either the written or oral rounds, let your sponsoring newspaper know right away. It is very important that you do this if you know of any reason that would cause you to have difficulty in reading, writing, getting to the microphone, understanding the pronouncer, or making the judges understand you. Make sure your sponsor or official escort informs the National Spelling Bee headquarters as soon as possible, or by the deadline listed in the rules, at the latest. Don't be embarrassed about doing this; bee officials will be sensitive and discreet. They will inform you privately of any special procedures that they or you will need to follow, and it's likely that other spellers and audience members will remain completely unaware that any accommodation is being made for you.

the tests are graded (they are scored electronically) and is selected so as to allow ninety or more spellers to advance to Round Three of the finals.

Spellers should keep in mind that Round Two gives them a chance to overcome a less-than-stellar performance in Round One. Each correctly spelled word in Round Two counts for three points. Therefore, if you miss a few items on the written test and spell your Round Two word correctly, you may qualify for Round Three, while another speller who misses the same number of items on the written test— or even one or two fewer—and misses the Round Two word may be eliminated.

Round One takes place in a very large room, usually the auditorium where the oral rounds of the bee are held. Spellers sit in assigned seats at long rows of tables. Each speller is given several No. 2 pencils, an eraser, a couple of blank sheets of paper, and a sealed envelope containing an official test form and an answer sheet with twenty-five multiple-choice items. The test form is preprinted with the speller's name and number. Spellers are allowed to bring extra No. 2 pencils and a sweater or jacket, but nothing else—no paper, purses, bags, or hats.

At the start of the round, the head judge instructs spellers to remove their test materials from the envelopes and check the identifying information. Then the pronouncer announces the start of a period of silence. This is the time to look over the items on the answer sheet and think about which words you know how to spell and which ones are a challenge.

For each word for which there are multiple spellings, the pronouncer will provide all the pronunciations listed in *Webster's Third*. He will also provide the part of speech, language of origin, definition, and a sentence. The pronouncer will pause for a few seconds, then repeat all of the information. No questions will be accepted from either the spellers or the audience. Spellers have five choices for each

The Written Round.

A Real Nail-Biter

"The first year I participated in the national finals, I was eleven years old. I was a little nervous and fidgety and had a terrible nail-biting habit. Well, a wire service photographer took a series of pictures of me doing things like scratching my eyebrow, biting my thumbnail, staring at the ceiling, and running my hand through my hair. That little series of four pictures ran in newspapers all over the country! I looked like a little blonde chimp, and I think my mother was a bit embarrassed. It taught me that what happens near a camera can be seen anywhere by nightfall, and I was much more careful after that."

—BARRIE TRINKLE,
*1973 National
Spelling Bee champion*

item and are given a reasonable amount of time to darken the circle corresponding to the correct choice. Then the pronouncer moves to the next item on the list. At the end of the list, the pronouncer will repeat the twenty-five items one more time and announce the start of another period of silence, during which spellers can check and change any answers.

The following tips should help you do well in the written round:

- Follow all directions.

- Don't open your test envelope until instructed to do so.

- Check to make sure you have the right test sheet; if not, raise your hand to let a staff member know immediately.

- Fill in the circles neatly; don't make stray marks on the paper.

- For each item, quickly eliminate the choices you know to be wrong, and choose from the remaining possible answers.

- You are allowed to change your answers at any time during the test period. Be sure to erase prior answers *completely*.

- Be careful! During the period of silence at the end of the test, you should check the answer sheet with the choices *and* your test form with the filled-in circles side by side. The written round is scored by computer, so accidentally skipping a line will throw off all the answers after it and could turn a threshold-breaking answer sheet into one that will not qualify you for Round Three.

- Obviously, you should not leave your seat without permission or talk to anyone during the written test. Don't risk disqualification!

Spellers will be allowed to leave the testing room but will not be allowed to return to complete the test. You should leave only in the direst emergency because doing so means that only the part of the test you have completed will be scored and you will likely be eliminated from the bee. The entire test takes about 45 minutes to an hour, so plan on remaining in your seat for that period of time.

What It's Like Onstage

Traditional oral spelling competition begins in Round Two. At some point on Wednesday of Bee Week, you will take your seat on the stage of the Scripps National Spelling Bee, take a deep breath, and wait for your Round Two word.

During most of your time onstage, you'll be sitting down. In the early rounds, there will be many spellers onstage. Round Two is completed

The American Dialect Society (ADS) was born in 1889, but has been voting on the "word of the year" only since 1990. However, ADS members Allan Metcalf and David Barnhart have researched the linguistic past and retroactively handed out "word of the year" awards to a new word every year since 1900, when the word of the year was "phony." Here's a sample:

1906: teddy bear
1928: athlete's foot
1938: teenager
1945: showbiz
1957: role model
1965: affirmative action
1976: couch potato
1989: virtual reality

Stay aware of your seatmates so you will know that you are sitting in the right place.

Lucky Charms

Don't hesitate to bring your rabbit's foot along to the competition. In fact, many spellers carry something to reassure them that all will turn out well, often something they happened to be wearing the first time they won a bee, like special T-shirts, bracelets, earrings, or socks. One speller confessed that she always has a small piece of craft putty in her pocket, because she had one there when she won her first school bee! Others carry items that were given to them specifically for good luck like shamrocks, horseshoe key chains, wishbones, or coins. All of those are fine. Just keep it small—no MP3 player or your lucky pocket dictionary!

in two segments. In 2006, there were 140 and 134 spellers onstage for each of the two segments of Round Two, 97 for each of Round Three, and 86 for Round Four. It may take as long as two hours to finish each of the early rounds.

There are flat risers on the stage, so each row of chairs is slightly higher than the one in front of it. This gives your parents a good view of you and photographers a better chance to take pictures. (It also means that you're always visible to everyone, so you will want to be aware of what your onstage behavior looks like! You

Theodore Yuan watches fellow competitors during Round Six of competition at the 2006 Scripps National Spelling Bee.

never know when your picture is being taken.) As each contestant spells, the next one or two contestants line up well behind him or her on the risers, out of the way but ready to move forward at the appropriate time.

A bee staffer will explain your path to the microphone. During longer breaks, staffers sometimes remove the extra chairs onstage and rearrange the remaining ones, so your path may change. Stay aware of your seatmates so you will know that you are sitting in the right place. Also, make sure your placard with the number on it is facing outward. This will help the judges and other bee staff keep everyone in order.

The auditorium can be chilly, especially first thing in the morning or if you're feeling a little nervous. Bring a light sweater or jacket.

Staying Sane

If you're feeling nervous on the morning of the competition, you should say so. Don't dwell on it, but let your family and friends know that you could use some encouragement. All the other spellers are feeling nervous too, even the "favorites." (In fact, they may feel more nervous, because they feel more pressure

Get Mental

"It's obvious that you need to have knowledge of word roots and language patterns in order to figure out unfamiliar words. Less obvious is the fact that you need to have poise and a mental routine in order to *apply* that knowledge to figuring out unfamiliar words. The worst mental state you can be in prior to participating in a spelling bee is the 'I sure hope I get words I know' mindset. You're best off accepting that you *are* going to get a word or words that are unfamiliar. If you expect the unfamiliar, you'll be more likely to become the word sleuth you know you can be."

—Paige Pipkin Kimble,
*1981 National
Spelling Bee champion*

to do well.) Experience and skill are no protection against butterflies in the stomach. If you put it out there in the open when you talk to other spellers and share a joke about it, you'll feel calmer.

Here are a few quick tips for competition day:

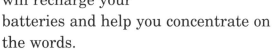

- Your best hedge against the jitteriness that affects your performance is plenty of sleep the night before. A good night's sleep will recharge your batteries and help you concentrate on the words.

- Don't pass up breakfast! Your brain needs food. If you're feeling too nervous to eat much, at least take a breakfast or energy bar with you and nibble it before you go onstage.

- Plan for success. Assume that you'll stay in the contest and will therefore be onstage for several hours. You will get some breaks; always take the opportunity to go to the restroom and get a drink before you return to your seat. Talk to your parents or legal guardian before the bee and arrange for them to have quick snacks ready for you during the breaks in case you feel

Don't try to absorb a big list of words at the last minute. The chance that you'll actually get one of those words is minuscule!

hungry. You won't be allowed to take food and drinks onstage.

- Don't try to absorb a big list of words at the last minute. The chance that you'll actually get one of those words is minuscule! Your time would be better spent meditating or talking to friends or enjoying some other pleasantly distracting activity that will help you relax and focus. (Some kids vouch that video games are great for this.)

Getting Your Parents to Chill

You can't do much to control your parents' feelings, but the calmer you are, the calmer they'll probably be. You might try giving them a small gift as a little joke before the bee: a fidget stone, worry beads, or a crochet hook and a ball of yarn. If they are really nervous, they might be better off not watching you

"Stationary" is being still while **"stationery"** is something you mail. Just remember that *stationary* has an a for *stay*, whereas *stationery* has an e for *envelope*.

Tip on the Slip from a Champ

"I am about as nervous as anyone onstage. I get distracted by the weird lighting, unfamiliar people and furniture, faces in the audience, and a lot of feelings that have no words for them. These are prime conditions for a slip of the tongue. No matter how many times you *think* the correct spelling in your brain, when it comes to actually vocalizing, your mouth may have a mind of its own. So here is what I did to avoid tragedy: I would rehearse the spelling in a quiet whisper, out loud but under my breath, a good distance away from the microphone. Then I would step up to the mike and do it again, louder. An immediate repetition of almost the same action has a pretty good chance of success. There is no perfect defense against slipping up, but I can say that, in four years of this kind of tight-rope walking, I never suffered the catastrophe of saying *g* for *j*."

—HENRY FELDMAN,
*1960 National
Spelling Bee champion*

Official Pronouncer Jacques Bailly, left, and Associate Pronouncer Dr. Brian Sietsema.

spell—at least not all the time. Let them know that it's okay for them to leave the auditorium, even when it's your turn. When they return, you can give them a discreet thumbs-up to let them know you are hanging in there just fine.

Probably the best thing you can do for someone who is nervous is to let this person do something for you. So put Mom or Dad in charge of something you need. Ask nicely if one of them would be willing to call a few of your friends after each round, get you your favorite beverage and have it ready when the round is over, or plan a special family outing for when the bee is over.

If you're with both parents and they're both nervous, take each of them aside separately before the bee starts and ask one to keep the other a little distracted.

A L T—ask, listen, think. Give yourself the best possible chance to spell the word correctly.

Your Turn to Spell

Sooner or later, it will be your turn to spell. Be sure to follow the instructions you were given about the flow of traffic onstage. Move to the microphone quickly and calmly, and adjust it so that you can speak into it easily without stooping or standing on tiptoe. Then watch the pronouncer give you your word.

Asking Questions

Asking good questions and listening carefully to the answers are two skills that a serious speller *must* develop. With so many competitors, the National Spelling Bee must place time constraints on them, so your time at the microphone is limited. Spend it wisely. Use the mnemonic **A L T—ask, listen, think.** Give yourself the best possible chance to spell the word correctly.

The official National Spelling Bee rules state the following:

> In oral competition, the speller may ask the pronouncer to pronounce the word again, define it, use it in a sentence, or provide the language origin. In addition, if the speller wishes to ask if the dictionary lists a specific root word as the root of the word to be spelled, the speller must specify a pronunciation of the root (not a

*D*o ask genuine questions you might have about the word you have been asked to spell, but *don't* ask questions just to call attention to yourself. The audience will smell show-off behavior from a mile away—and find it annoying.

Moreover, in national competition, asking unnecessary questions or making observations to draw attention to yourself eats away at your valuable time limit at the microphone. Familiarize yourself with Rule 11 of the Contest Rules of the Scripps National Spelling Bee, which begins: "A speller is expected to spell familiar words without delay and to refrain from routines that employ unnecessary or repetitive questioning." This rule spells out the amount of time national finalists have at the microphone. Familiarity with the details of this rule is extremely important for national finalists. See the complete rule at www.spellingbee.com.

Even though the rules don't require it—you should *always* pronounce the word you are given.

More Words of the Year

The American Dialect Society has designated the following words as the "word of the year":

1903: highbrow
1920: normalcy
1921: media
1937: groovy
1949: cool
1967: ripoff
1977: loony tunes
1985: rocket scientist
1992: not!

spelling), its language, and its definition. . . . A speller is expected to spell familiar words without delay and to refrain from routines that employ unnecessary or repetitive questioning.

When they get a word they think they know, some spellers launch into the spelling immediately. This practice is very risky, because a speller who mistakes one easy word for another and spells the wrong word will hear the dreaded *ding!* of the judges' bell.

When you first receive your word, you should mentally center yourself. Take a deep breath if you need to. Then repeat the word clearly into the microphone, facing

the judges and using the exact pronunciation that was given. This helps them know that you have heard your word correctly. If *you* are not sure whether you've heard it correctly, ask the pronouncer to re-pronounce the word.

Probably no one in your life will listen to your every utterance as closely as the National Spelling Bee judges will. There's nothing that makes them feel worse than the plight of a speller who has inserted an extra syllable, misunderstood the sound /th/ as /f/, or simply spelled the wrong word, even though the responsibility of making sure of the pronunciation belongs to the speller. You must give the judges a reasonable chance to correct you, so— even though the rules don't require it—you should *always* pronounce the word you are given. If the judges think you have mispronounced the word, they will ask you to pronounce it again. If they still believe you are not saying the word correctly, they will ask the pronouncer to pronounce it again for you. If this happens, you should listen very carefully, then re-pronounce the word into the microphone, just as the pronouncer gave it to you. Once everyone is satisfied that you are saying the word correctly, you can get down to the business of figuring out the correct spelling.

Stephanie Baer spells her first word in the 2003 National Spelling Bee.

Can You Spell "Life Lesson"?

"Looking back, as hard as it is to believe, I am glad I did not win—because I learned lessons I badly needed to learn through not obtaining my goal. You see, my mistake in 1996 was not that I didn't know how to spell the word **dispel**. It was that I thought I knew how to spell everything. . . . I now understand that humility is what makes an accomplishment worthwhile. If you don't expect to win, the surprise of doing so is all the more rewarding. And if you don't win but have a humble attitude from the start, disappointment is minimized and you can focus on others rather than on yourself. This lesson has made the rest of my life, up to this point, much happier than the hours following my elimination from the 1996 National Spelling Bee."

—CORRIE LOEFFLER,
National Spelling Bee finalist, 1994, 1995, and 1996; press desk, Scripps National Spelling Bee

When you first receive your word, you should mentally center yourself.

Word Mystery: The Curious Case of the Missing C

Many words from Romance languages (French, Spanish, Italian, Portuguese, and Catalan) have Latin roots, but their spelling may have changed. For example, **brocade** comes from Spanish, Catalan, and Italian words, and further back from the Latin word *broccus*, meaning "projecting (like a tooth)." How it lost the extra *c* is a mystery to which the dictionary entry alone offers no solution.

Remember: *Ask, listen, think.* Sometimes spellers are a little shell-shocked when they receive a word they've never heard, so they'll go through the motions of asking questions—but the answers go in one ear and out the other. Again, mentally center yourself, and tell yourself that you *can* figure out this word.

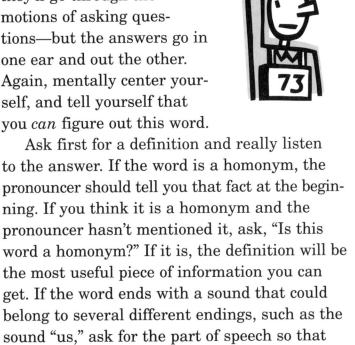

Ask first for a definition and really listen to the answer. If the word is a homonym, the pronouncer should tell you that fact at the beginning. If you think it is a homonym and the pronouncer hasn't mentioned it, ask, "Is this word a homonym?" If it is, the definition will be the most useful piece of information you can get. If the word ends with a sound that could belong to several different endings, such as the sound "us," ask for the part of speech so that you know whether it might be an adjective ending in *-ous* or a noun ending in *-us*. Asking for a sentence lets you hear the word in context, which is just one more piece of insurance. If you feel sure of the word, you can now safely spell it.

However, if you're not entirely sure you know the word, you should next ask for the language of origin. This can help you figure out some letter combinations quickly. For example, knowing that *pharos* comes from Greek will help you spell the /f/ phoneme with a *ph*. (See Chapters 3 and 4 for more on language origins and spelling patterns.)

If you think the word may contain a particular root, you may ask, but you must know from what language it is and what it means. This question is most useful when you are trying to decide between two or more possible spellings, as when there is an unstressed syllable containing a schwa. Phrase your question something like this: "Does *nectariferous* contain the Greek combining form *-phor,* meaning "bearing"? The pronouncer will check the dictionary entry and

The judges confer.

Rich in Words

"Your mind is like your body: It needs to be exercised to keep in shape. Learning and memorizing words has helped to keep my mind fit. I've added many of those words I learned for the spelling bee to my vocabulary. I still use them, and they've made me a better journalist and a better writer. Learning a word makes it yours—exactly like putting money in your pocket— and it makes you rich in a way that money can't."

PATT MORRISON,
National Spelling Bee finalist, 1966; Los Angeles Times *columnist, Emmy-winning television host, PBS and NPR commentator*

Sports and Games

LEVEL: Advanced

avalement
baccarat
bagatelle
barbotte
bezique
cayenne
chouette
coliseum
derailleur
fianchetto
gymkhana
klaberjass
kriegspiel
lansquenet
luger
mistigris
polignac
pugilist
quoits
rangdoodles
rebote
roleo
salchow
schussboomer
snipsnapsnorum
spinnaker
tailleur
tobogganer
toxophilite
trainasium
troco
Yarborough

give you an answer. Sometimes the answer will be "No" or "I don't see that listed here." Keep trying. "Does it contain the Latin combining form *-fer,* meaning 'bearing'?" Remember that a "no" answer does not *necessarily* mean that you are on the wrong track with the spelling. Sometimes the root you've asked about doesn't come from the language you indicated or doesn't mean what you think, and the pronouncer has no choice but to answer your question in the negative. Remember: Diligent root-word study often pays off big-time!

While you are entitled to ask questions, you should always remember that you are subject to a time limit that is strictly enforced. If you waste time in unnecessary pursuits—for example, trying to extract an unnatural pronunciation from the pronouncer in order to guess at the spelling of a schwa— you may exhaust your time limit and be forced to spell the word imme- diately. Once you have done this, you may be subject to a shorter time limit for subsequent rounds.

Stuck in the Middle with *U*

The Scripps National Spelling Bee has a time-honored rule that many other spelling bees also follow: Even after hav- ing started to spell, a speller is allowed to stop

Pretend that the rest of the audience is on Mars, and that you and the judges are sitting in your living room having a conversation.

and start over, retracing the spelling from the beginning, as long as there is *no change* to the letters that were already spelled or the order they were given in.

Have you ever gotten lost in the middle of spelling a word? It happens all the time. Many people get confused when they stop to think about the next letter or syllable, so if you hesitate on a spelling for more than a few seconds, it's a good idea to start over and spell the word all the way through. Do let the judges know

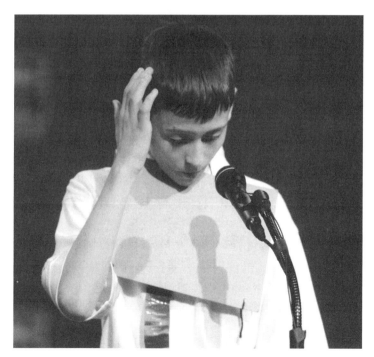

Ask. Listen. Think.

Have you ever heard anyone spell the word *Mississippi* "*M - i* - crooked letter - crooked letter - *i* - crooked letter - crooked letter - *i* - humpback - humpback - *i*"? Your grandparents probably know that jingle! Perhaps you have heard "*M - i* - double *s - i* - double *s - i* - double *p - i*."

P-l-e-a-s-e don't spell double letters this way in a spelling bee! The judges will expect you to spell each letter separately, and if you don't, you are likely to confuse yourself as well as them. Also, you'd be in deep trouble if you tried to spell a word like *vacuum* or *muumuu* by saying "double *u*"!

A word beginning with the /k/ sound is statistically more likely to be spelled with the letter c than with the letter k.

Sussing It Out

Sometimes you can figure out a word using word roots that you know, but there are times when the best you can do is guess at the spelling using whatever mental associations you have. Anurag Kashyap, 2005 National Spelling Bee champion, and a maestro of both techniques:

"At the nationals, I successfully spelled **priscilla, pompier,** and **ornithorhynchous** despite not studying the words. I correctly guessed **priscilla** by thinking of Priscilla Presley. **Pompier** means something to do with firefighters, so I thought of the fiery volcano at Pompeii, and remembered that the 'ee-yay' sound in French is *-ier*. I guessed **ornithorhynchous** using the Greek roots of *ornithos*, 'bird,' and *rhynchos*, 'beak.'

that you are starting the word over, and if you want to be especially cautious, wait for a nod from them. Waiting for the judges' acknowledgment of your plan is not necessary, but it is a safety measure. It makes crystal clear what letter sequence you want the judges to use when they evaluate your spelling.

The Judges

The judges at the National Spelling Bee typically have many years of experience. Some of them have served as regional spelling bee judges for years before moving up to the national level, and others have served the National Spelling Bee in other capacities before becoming judges. They are very good at what they do, which is understanding spellers—even those with strong national or regional accents, quiet voices, or speech impediments. However, you should always keep in mind that the judges are the *most* important people in the room to communicate with. The easier you can make

their job, the less chance there is that you will have to endure an agonizing delay as they try to determine whether you gave the correct spelling.

Pretend that the rest of the audience is on Mars and that you and the judges are sitting in your living room having a conversation. Look straight at them when you spell, speak as clearly as you can, and don't hesitate to address them directly: "Judges, am I saying the word correctly?" or "I'm going to start my spelling over now, okay?" Doing this will not only get you the information you need, but will also help you feel in charge of your time at the microphone. And that can boost your confidence, which can get you through some majorly tough words.

Using Your Instinct: KISS

et's imagine for a moment that you are standing at the microphone on the National Spelling Bee stage and you have just been given a word that you have never heard before. You inquire about the word's meaning and its origin. You rule out all root words that seem like possibilities. Not a single

Can Do

"I competed in the National Spelling Bee twice, and both times I thought it was the most unusual and interesting week of my life. I expected everyone to be just like me. Instead, I met more than a hundred kids who shared my love of words, but were different from me in so many ways that sometimes I forgot exactly why we had all come to Washington that week. Years later, I realized that the best lesson I got from being a contestant was that what you *can* do well is far more important than what you can't."

—VICTOR HASTINGS, *National Spelling Bee finalist, 1973 and 1974; attorney*

Behind the Scenes

There are many people working at a National Spelling Bee, although spellers can see only a few of them from the stage. The press desk, the records desk, the sound recording table, the Comfort Room, and other positions are busy all the time during the spelling. These positions are often staffed by former spellers. So take comfort in knowing that there are many people present who know exactly how you're feeling onstage and are working to make your bee experience the best it can be.

answer to your questions gives you even a hint of a clue. In a nutshell, you know absolutely nothing about this word.

What should you do? Consider employing the KISS rule—Keep It Simple (for) Success. Just spell the word the way it sounds as simply as you can—no fancy spins or silent letters thrown in.

You will have to use your own judgment about what KISS means to you. Some people might go ahead and spell the word completely phonetically, and they might be right. However, English has certain common spelling patterns that aren't phonetic. For example, a word beginning with the /k/ sound is statistically more likely to be spelled with the letter c than with the letter k. So you may want to work out a commonsense approach, using a combination of phonetics and well-known spelling patterns. For any given word, you might be wrong, but you could just as easily be right.

If you are leery about this, observe a spelling bee and test it out. You can visit another school's spelling bee, a regional spelling bee, a corporate spelling bee, or just watch a National Spelling Bee rerun on television. Spell silently along with the other spellers as they receive their words. Use the KISS rule when there is no information that can help you with the correct spelling of the word. Tally how many times your spelling is

One of the best things you can do for yourself is to think about what it will be like when you miss a word.

right when you use the KISS rule and how many times your spelling is wrong when you use it. Then you can decide for yourself whether this approach will be effective for you.

In the end, all you really have to go on for a "mystery word" is your instinct. It's best to have tested your crunch-time instinct before you need it!

What Happens If You Miss a Word?

We all know the first sign of having missed a word: *Ding!* If you happen to be the speller, first you'll hear the head judge ring a bell. Then the pronouncer will give the correct spelling. A National Spelling Bee staff member (often a former national finalist) will then greet you and walk offstage with you to the Comfort Room, a special lounge for spellers who have been eliminated. Your parents are allowed to meet you there, if you want them to. You can stay in the Comfort Room as long as you like—sitting in the comfy chairs, looking up your word in the dictionary, eating snacks,

Spelling bees are no longer just for kids. Bee fever has caught on in bars and clubs across the country. One Brooklyn, New York, bar even holds bimonthly bees, thanks to the successful combination of alcohol and orthography. Though the atmosphere lacks the formality and suspense of a National Spelling Bee, adult spellers still face fierce competition and—ahem—a **cornucopia** of challenging words. The grownups win free drinks, not college scholarships, which means the more **bibulous** participants may get a little sloppy as the evening wears on.

The chance that the pronouncer has mispronounced a word in the National Spelling Bee finals is almost nil.

and chatting with staff members and other eliminated spellers. If you feel more than a little upset, the Comfort Room staff will make sure you have tissues, a shoulder to cry on, and privacy and quiet. You can leave the Comfort Room whenever you are ready. It's possible that a member of the news media will be outside in the hallway and will ask to talk to you about your bee participation. The bee encourages you to speak with this individual if you choose. This is your fifteen minutes of fame!

Some spellers who make it to the national finals have never missed a spelling word in

W-H-E-E-L-B-A-R-R-O-W:
Finalists at play.

competition. If you are such a speller, take a moment to imagine that bell ringing for you, because it most likely will. Every speller who makes it to the National Spelling Bee finals dreams of winning, but one of the best things you can do for yourself is to think about what it will be like when you miss a word. You will still be disappointed when it happens, but you'll be able to bounce back emotionally and enjoy the rest of the week with your new friends if you've prepared yourself to hear that *ding!*

Appealing: When, Why, and How

n appeal of the judges' decision is the responsibility of your parent(s) or legal guardian. Appeals are usually made if the speller can show that there is an accepted alternate spelling or if the pronouncer gave the speller a homonym but did not clarify that it was a homonym. If you feel that you correctly spelled a version of the word that the pronouncer gave you—and the pronouncer did not give you a meaning of the word you were to spell—an appeal is in order. Ask an adult who has accompanied you to go to the judges before it would be your turn to spell again if you were

The Fundamentals

" A newspaper reporter asked me how I felt. I said, 'T-I-R-E-D.' The National Spelling Bee has a physical endurance component in addition to the intellectual component. Generally, the simple rules apply. Get a good night's sleep. Eat a good breakfast and lunch. And whenever there's a bathroom break, take advantage of it, even if you don't think you need to."

—JON PENNINGTON, *1986 National Spelling Bee champion*

Where are they now?

As you might expect, National Spelling Bee champions typically go on to succeed in other areas. Many have become doctors, attorneys, teachers, engineers, journalists, university professors, and business executives. The 1941 champion, Louis Edward Sissman (1928–1976), was a celebrated poet. His book *Hello, Darkness* won the National Book Critics Circle Award for poetry in 1978. Below are some of the professions practiced by champions of the last half century.

1951	Irving Belz	Psychiatrist, Conroe, Texas
1954	William Cashore	Professor of pediatrics, Brown University School of Medicine, Providence, Rhode Island
1960	Henry Feldman	Medical statistician, Boston, Massachusetts
1961	John Capehart	Thoracic surgeon, Dallas, Texas
1971	Jonathan Knisely	Physician and associate professor of radiology at Yale University School of Medicine, New Haven, Connecticut
1972	Robin Kral	Biotechnology executive, Dallas, Texas
1973	Barrie Trinkle	Editor and writer, Seattle, Washington

still in the bee. Follow the bee's guidelines about filing appeals. This is applicable to any spelling bee. At the National Spelling Bee, your parent or legal guardian will need to fill out a paper form explaining the disagreement with the judges' decision.

Appeals have rarely resulted in the reinstatement of a speller, so don't waste time with a frivolous appeal. If you appeal your elimination, you will be reinstated *only* if the judges decide that you have correctly spelled an acceptable form of the word you were given. You will not be reinstated if you misunderstood the word

1974	Julie Ann Junkin Bedsole	Third-grade teacher, Northport, Alabama
1977	John Paola	Veterinarian, Annapolis, Maryland
1978	Peg McCarthy	Psychologist, Topeka, Kansas
1979	Katie Kerwin McCrimmon	Reporter, *Rocky Mountain News,* Denver, Colorado
1980	Jacques Bailly	Associate professor of classics, University of Vermont; Scripps National Spelling Bee pronouncer
1981	Paige Pipkin Kimble	Director, Scripps National Spelling Bee, Cincinnati, Ohio
1983	Blake Giddens	Civil engineer, Alexandria, Virginia; Scripps National Spelling Bee judge
1985	Balu Natarajan	Sports medicine physician, Chicago, Illinois
1986	Jon Pennington	Editor, Arlington, Virginia
1987	Stephanie Petit	Attorney, San Francisco, California
1988	Rageshree Ramachandran	Physician and medical researcher, San Francisco, California
1991	Joanne Lagatta	Physician, Chicago, Illinois
1992	Amanda Goad	Attorney, New York, New York
1996	Wendy Guey	Investor relations associate, New York, New York

and spelled a different word! It is *always* your—and only your—responsibility to make sure you have understood your word.

Occasionally, spellers appeal on the basis of the pronouncer's having "mispronounced" the word. This kind of appeal is also doomed to failure. The pronouncer can give only pronunciations listed in *Webster's Third New International Dictionary.* Sometimes spellers are accustomed to hearing a nonstandard pronunciation and are confused by the dictionary pronunciations, or their dictionaries may list pronunciations that *Webster's Third* doesn't have. That's too bad, but that argument won't get a speller back into the bee: What *Webster's Third* says goes. And by the time of the national finals, the pronouncer has pronounced every word on the list many times and at least twice in front of other officials and word panelists. The chance that the pronouncer has mispronounced a word in the National Spelling Bee finals is almost nil.

So now you may be wondering what constitutes an "accepted alternate spelling." The official rules of the National Spelling Bee state:

Samir Sudhir Patel gets it right in Round Six of the 2006 National Spelling Bee.

Webster's Third New International Dictionary and its addenda section . . . shall serve as the final authority for the spelling of words. If more than one spelling is listed for a word that the pronouncer has provided for the speller to spell, any of these spellings shall be accepted as correct if all of the following three criteria are met: *(1) The pronunciations of the words are identical, (2) the definitions of the words are identical,* and *(3) the words are clearly identified as being standard variants of each other.* Spellings at other locations having temporal labels (such as *archaic, obsolete*), stylistic labels (such as *substand, nonstand*), or regional labels (such as *North, Midland, Irish*) that differ from main entry spellings not having these status labels shall not be accepted as correct.

For example, both *broccoli* and *brocoli* would be acceptable spellings but *abbaye* (an archaic variant of *abbey*), *thoro* (a nonstandard spelling of *thorough*), and *cieling* (an obsolete variant of *ceiling*) would not.

Realistically, it's not likely that you'll see words like these in the National Spelling Bee— the word panel tends not to include words with alternate spellings on the list—but now you know what kinds of alternate spellings are defensible.

Great Rewards

"Right after spelling the winning word, I was totally stunned and I felt as if I were the luckiest person on Earth. I remember thinking that I would be able to sit on a dais with all of the top spellers at the awards banquet, and that was such a big reward to me. Nothing else registered until later because I was so shocked at the time!"

—NUPUR LALA, *1999 National Spelling Bee champion*

A Journalist Is Born

"At the press conference after I won, the reporters asked what I wanted to be when I grew up. I spontaneously answered that I wanted to be a journalist. I think I sensed the excitement of covering an event like the bee. I eventually became a reporter for my sponsoring newspaper, the *Rocky Mountain News*."

—KATIE KERWIN MCCRIMMON, *1979 National Spelling Bee champion* (winning word: **maculature**)

When It's Down to a Few, Then Two

Often, there is a short break when there are only a few spellers left, and parents of these spellers are invited to take a seat at the side of the stage. A speller who misses in these higher rounds will join his or her parents in these seats rather than leaving the stage. This way, it is easy for spellers to be reinstated into the bee if all of the spellers in a single round misspell their word, and it is also easier for the media to interview and take pictures of top finalists and their families at the end of the bee.

When there are two spellers remaining in the National Spelling Bee, the rules become slightly more complex. Prior to 1991, when one of the two remaining spellers misspelled a word, the other speller had to spell that word correctly plus one more to win the championship. This rule could be somewhat problematic because the second speller, having eliminated one spelling possibility, was often able to guess the spelling correctly even if he or she had never heard the word. Moreover, the speller with the lower placard number of the two remaining spellers had to correctly spell three more words than the second-place speller in order to win, while the speller with the higher placard number had to produce only two more correctly spelled words than the other speller.

Nowadays, the rule has been adjusted and simplified: When one of the two remaining spellers misses a word, the other speller is given the next word on the list rather than the misspelled word, and the winning speller must correctly spell two more words than the second-place speller, regardless of their relative positions onstage. So if speller number 21 spells correctly and speller number 137 misses a word in Round Nineteen, speller number 21 is given an entirely new word in Round Twenty and need spell only that word to win the bee.

2005 National champion Anurag Kashyap spells it out.

Match These

English has borrowed onomatopoeic words from many languages. Can you match these words to their meaning and language of origin?

1. cachinnate (Latin)
2. flicflac (French)
3. clinquant (Middle French)
4. rataplan (French)
5. ululate (Latin)
6. reboant (Latin)

a. to laugh usually loudly or convulsively
b. glittering especially with gold decoration
c. to utter a loud mournful usually protracted and rhythmical sound
d. reverberating
e. a brushing movement of the foot used in ballet as a connecting step
f. the iterative sound of beating

Some local and regional bees still use the older rule, so it is good to understand it thoroughly.

Before 1991, if there were 150 spellers in the National Spelling Bee, the first speller to miss a word got 150th place, the second got 149th place, and so on. Now, in the interest of fairness, all spellers who are eliminated in the same round are considered to have tied for the same place and therefore receive the same prize. In 2005, Samir Patel and Aliya Deri tied for second place behind champion Anurag Kashyap—the first time two spellers have shared that spot.

Head-to-Head Contests

In the first few decades of the National Spelling Bee, when the word lists were easier, it wasn't terribly uncommon for two spellers to battle for many rounds before one was declared champion. In fact, there were three years—1950, 1957, and 1962—in which the word list was exhausted

and co-champions were declared.

Nowadays, long head-to-head contests are rare once the contestants have been whittled to two, but in 1997, Rebecca Sealfon of New York City and Prem Trivedi of Howell, New Jersey, spelled against each other for eight rounds for the National Spelling Bee title. Here are their round results:

Round Fifteen:
Prem Trivedi: usufructuary
Rebecca Sealfon: niello
Round Sixteen:
Prem: supererogatory
Rebecca: duenna
Round Seventeen:
Prem: analemma (misspelled as *annalemma*)
Rebecca: dulcinea (misspelled as *dulcenilla*)
Round Eighteen:
Prem: holophytic
Rebecca: sufflaminate
Round Nineteen:
Prem: foudroyant
Rebecca: deliquesce
Round Twenty:
Prem: philhellene
Rebecca: bourgade
Round Twenty-One:
Prem: griffonage
Rebecca: anglophilia
Round Twenty-Two:
Prem: cortile (misspelled as *cortille*)
Rebecca: coterie
Round Twenty-Three:
Rebecca: euonym

In 2006, Katharine "Kerry" Close of Spring Lake, New Jersey, and Finola Mei Hwa Hackett of Tofield, Alberta, Canada, also battled for eight rounds. Kerry won the championship with *Ursprache*.

Chomping Champ

"I chewed gum to calm my nerves a bit during the contest, but didn't have a chance to spit it out or swallow it after I won. That led to several widely published, rather embarrassing pictures of me holding the trophy, mouth wide open as I prepared to take another furious chomp on my gum. Adrenaline got the best of me."

—ROBIN KRAL,
1972 National Spelling Bee champion
(winning word: **macerate**)

Practice Makes Perfect

"I repeated the word **antediluvian** (after spelling it). Judge Mary Brooks said, 'That is correct.' Someone cheered; in hindsight, it was probably my mother. I felt as if an electric current was running through me, as if my body was an electromagnet being drawn downward toward the ground, and it required all my strength to simply keep standing up. Scripps' Bill Burleigh handed me the trophy, and I knew exactly what I was going to do with it: one hand on the base, one hand wrapped around the back of the cup, arms in the air. I admit it: At home in my bedroom, I had practiced imitating—and improving upon—the winners in photos from *Words of the Champions* and *Bee Week Guides* of bygone years. I never expected to be one of them."

—NED ANDREWS,
*1994 National
Spelling Bee champion*

Winning

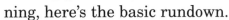

If you're one of the last few spellers onstage, you'll be concentrating on the words so hard that you probably won't give any thought to what will happen at the end of the bee. So, just to prepare you for the distant but enticing possibility of winning, here's the basic rundown.

Once the last word has been spelled, there will be a lot of noise. The champion will be presented the trophy, and the winner's parents will likely present some hugs and kisses! A TV reporter will probably interview the winner for the TV cameras, and many, many pictures will be taken.

If you win, you should expect to be busy for a while. Everyone understands that you've been under a lot of pressure for the previous few hours, and that you may feel very emotional. Take a few moments to compose yourself and ask for a glass of water or some tissues if you need them.

It's exciting and sometimes a little scary to be interviewed by so many people. If you're that lucky speller, you may find that things will go more easily in your exhilarated state if you're ready for a few obvious questions you will certainly be asked—how you studied, whether you knew all the words you got, what you want to be when you grow up, and what you plan to do with the prize money.

The winner and his or her parents often spend much of the day (and night) that follow the bee in television studios or on the telephone, but somehow, in the midst of all that excitement, the winner also finds time to prepare a short speech for the awards banquet. If the National Spelling Bee finals are the climax of the week, the awards banquet is its denouement (a good word to add to your spelling bee notebook!). It's a memorable evening of fun, companionship, delicious food, and heartfelt thank-yous to the parents, coaches, and sponsors who made a first-place finish at the National Spelling Bee possible.

2006 winner, Kerry Close, gets ready for her close-up. This was the first year the National Spelling Bee was broadcast on primetime televison.

Subtlety and Specificity

"The legacy has been an appreciation for subtlety and specificity, for taking care to use the right word the right way. Understanding how words are constructed, how they're related, how easily you can misunderstand them—all this I came to appreciate as I crammed for the contests. I'm no grammar snob, despite my career as a copy editor. But I appreciate simple, direct communication."

—DARIENNE HOSLEY
STEWART, *National Spelling Bee finalist, 1985; copy editor*

What's Next?

After Bee Week is over and you've gone home, you'll have some thinking to do. If this was your last year to compete, it's time to kick back, enjoy your summer, and start looking for a new challenge! Your hard work and your ability to stand up under pressure will have long-term benefits that you'll continue to reap even after you've put your spelling notebook on the shelf and turned to rock climbing, integral calculus, superhero training, or whatever your next bold undertaking is.

If (1) you didn't win the National Spelling Bee this year, (2) you won't turn sixteen or finish the eighth grade before next year's national finals, and (3) your local sponsor will allow you to compete again, ask yourself: Did I learn a lot? Was it fun? Do I want to come back and improve my ranking next year? If the answers are "Yes," give yourself a big pat on the back—then put your good buddy, the dictionary, where you can get to it easily.

After all, there are only about 362 days until the next National Spelling Bee. . . .

CHAPTER 7

Playable Words

ou've probably already enjoyed multiplayer games like Scrabble, Boggle, or Balderdash, or solo word activities like crosswords, cryptograms, or anagrams. There's something particularly satisfying about learning a new word this way, which makes it more likely that you'll remember and use it. There's an excellent chance you'll remember the words you learn in the puzzles that follow, because although some are easy, you'll have to work pretty hard to solve others. You're definitely going to want a dictionary nearby.

Don't forget to add new words to your spelling notebook!

Add Diction

The object here is to start with the letters at the top and add letters from the list at the bottom to complete five words. Each word builds on the letters of the word before it. The order of the existing letters will not change, but new letters can be inserted into the middle of the word or added to either end.

Puzzle #1

S I

— — — Religious offense

— — — — Warble

— — — — — Employing

— — — — — — One form of school transportation

— — — — — — — Putting to an improper use

U A N B G

Puzzle #2

O N

— — — Charged particle

— — — — Regal animal

— — — — — — Principal unit of the Roman army

— — — — — — — — Embassy

— — — — — — — — — — Assertion

G L L I E T A A

Puzzle #3

I L

— — — Feel sick

— — — — Hammer's target

— — — — — Slow creature

— — — — — — — Like a serpent

— — — — — — — — With sarcasm

Y N R A S K

Puzzle #4

H O

— — — Monopolize

— — — — Kong

— — — — — — Wishing

— — — — — — — Jumping

— — — — — — — — Type of mall

P S N P G I

Puzzle #5

D D

— — — Took action

— — — — Expired

— — — — — Plunged headfirst

— — — — — — — Separated

— — — — — — — — Stockholder's reward

I V I E D N

Puzzle #6

I E

_ _ _ Deceive

_ _ _ _ Food label fad word

_ _ _ _ _ Metric measure

_ _ _ _ _ _ One who catalogues

_ _ _ _ _ _ _ Get too much sun

T L B R S

Puzzle #7

O B

_ _ _ Hold up

_ _ _ _ Dressing gown

_ _ _ _ _ Investigate

_ _ _ _ _ _ _ Kind of court

_ _ _ _ _ _ _ _ _ Exploratory

T E R V P A I

Puzzle #8

N D

_ _ _ Moreover

_ _ _ _ Hourglass filler

_ _ _ _ _ Reviewing platform

_ _ _ _ _ _ Unit of hair

_ _ _ _ _ _ _ _ Beached

E S A T D R

Puzzle #9

R E

__ __ __ Regret

__ __ __ __ Bumpkin

__ __ __ __ __ Muscovite money

__ __ __ __ __ __ Gang event

__ __ __ __ __ __ __ Disintegrate

M L C U B

Puzzle #10

A E

__ __ __ Flying hero

__ __ __ __ "Chantilly _____"

__ __ __ __ __ Cavalry weapon

__ __ __ __ __ __ __ Decorative drape

__ __ __ __ __ __ __ __ Landslide

H A L V A C N

"Bumpkin *originally comes from a Dutch word for 'small cask,'* bommekijn."

Dictionary Devil

T he Dictionary Devil has mixed up these words and their meanings. Even worse, he's taken some words from the definitions and jumbled them at the bottom of each puzzle. The Dictionary Devil thinks he's pretty clever. But he's not as clever as you. Match the words to the definitions and fill in the blanks from the words at the bottom of each puzzle.

Puzzle #1

angstrom ___
(1) an unusually short _____

baccarat ___
(2) lamentation, _____

pegasus ___
(3) a unit of _____ equal to one ten-billionth of a _____

homily ___
(4) a _____ _____ horse

quadruped ___
(5) a _____ game played especially in _____ casinos

picayune ___
(6) a show of daring or _____

plaint ___
(7) an _____ having four feet

bravura ___
(8) something _____

brilliance European sermon meter
animal trivial fabulous wail length winged card

P u z z l e #2

crenation ___
(1) a long _____ marked usually by many _____ of fortune

funicular ___
(2) any of a _____ of small swift slender dogs that are used for

_____

loge ___
(3) one of the rounded _____ on an edge (as of a coin)

marquetry ___
(4) a small _____

macle ___
(5) _____ work of wood, shell, or _____ (as on a table or cabinet)

odyssey ___
(6) a twinned _____

quarto ___
(7) a cable_____ ascending a _____

whippet ___
(8) the size of a piece of _____ cut four from a _____

**railway inlaid racing mountain changes breed compartment
ivory crystal wandering paper projections sheet**

Puzzle #3

audit ___
(1) a pointed witty _____

vesicant ___
(2) a _____ horse or _____

zinger ___
(3) an agent that causes _____

acknowledgment ___
(4) a _____ preparation used in styling _____

depot ___
(5) a _____ of anxiety, apprehension, or _____

angst ___
(6) _____

mousse ___
(7) a _____ examination and _____

pinto ___
(8) a thing done or _____ in recognition of something _____

**review remark pony foamy insecurity spotted methodical
feeling given hair storehouse received blistering**

Puzzle #4

abjection ___
(1) a _____ chain or _____ hanging between two points

peer ___
(2) separation or _____ into two parts or connected _____

festoon ___
(3) a fictitious _____

pseudonym ___
(4) any of the _____ of various carnivorous _____ (as a dog)

remuda ___
(5) one that is of _____ standing with _____

seine ___
(6) the herd of _____ from which those to be used for the day are chosen

bifurcation ___
(7) a low or downcast _____

whelp ___
(8) a large _____ _____ net

**another   young   weighted   segments   strip   state   mammals
branching   decorative   equal   name   horses   fishing**

Puzzle #5

firebrand ___
(1) an interrogative _____ or clause

tundra ___
(2) a young _____

visage ___
(3) a _____ plain of arctic and subarctic _____

question ___
(4) a professional _____ of epic _____

mithridate ___
(5) _____

butte ___
(6) an _____ against _____

cygnet ___
(7) the _____ or countenance of a _____ or sometimes an animal

rhapsodist ___
(8) an isolated steep _____

**person   poems   hill   swan   poison   sentence   reciter   treeless
agitator   antidote   regions   face**

Puzzle #6

unabridged ___
(1) of very high _____

deprecatory ___
(2) marked by _____ enthusiasm and often intense uncritical

_____

superlative ___
(3) _____

edentulous ___
(4) contemptuously _____ of _____ nature and motives

eloquent ___
(5) being the most _____ of its _____

synthetic ___
(6) _____ to avert _____

cynical ___
(7) _____ or movingly _____ or revealing

fanatic ___
(8) produced _____

**distrustful   devotion   class   toothless   quality   excessive   human
vividly   complete   approval   seeking   artificially   expressive**

Puzzle #7

pastiche ___
(1) disagreeably _____ or _____

debutante ___
(2) a _____ made of _____ from different works

plaiting ___
(3) a small _____ sockeye salmon

raucous ___
(4) a very large swift-footed _____ _____ of Africa and Arabia

ostrich ___
(5) _____ _____ and enthusiasm

vim ___
(6) a man holding a rank of honor below a _____ but above a

_____

kokanee ___
(7) a young _____ making her _____ entrance into society

baronet ___
(8) the _____ of strands

**robust   bird   selections   energy   baron   formal   knight   harsh
flightless   interlacing   composition   landlocked   woman   strident**

Puzzle #8

trilby ___
(1) a _____ turn used for altering the direction of hill descent

christie ___
(2) a green or _____ _____ that forms on copper, brass, or bronze

populace ___
(3) pasta made in long _____ _____ smaller in diameter than spaghetti

vermicelli ___
(4) a woman's _____ room, bedroom, or _____ sitting room

proclivity ___
(5) an inclination or _____ toward _____

boudoir ___
(6) the _____ of fat from the back of a hog cured by _____ and salting

fatback ___
(7) the _____ people

verdigris ___
(8) a soft _____ hat with indented crown

**deposit   common   felt   strings   solid   dressing   skiing   tendency
something   strip   private   drying   bluish**

Puzzle #9

kudu ___
(1) a large or _____ _____

tendency ___
(2) a sauce made _____ of oil, vinegar, and _____

gourmand ___
(3) _____ repartee

gaff ___
(4) a _____ to a _____ kind of thought or action

badinage ___
(5) a _____ used to take fish or turtles

apocalypse ___
(6) one who is excessively _____ of eating and _____

tome ___
(7) a grayish brown African _____ with large spirally twisted horns

vinaigrette ___
(8) a writing prophesying a _____ in which _____ forces are destroyed

**fond   evil   typically   antelope   drinking   seasonings   particular
book   proneness   playful   cataclysm   spear   scholarly**

Puzzle #10

tirade ___
(1) a _____ _____ with a curved blade and thick back

biotite ___
(2) a man practicing the _____ _____

saber ___
(3) a dark _____ containing _____, magnesium, potassium, and aluminum

warlock ___
(4) a _____ purplish-blue _____

affenpinscher ___
(5) ground _____

carabid ___
(6) a place, scene, or state of _____ and confusion

sapphire ___
(7) a _____ speech of _____ or condemnation

bedlam ___
(8) any of a breed of _____ dogs with a wiry black, red, tan, or gray coat

**mica   small   dark   prolonged   arts   cavalry   uproar   black   abuse
color   iron   beetle   sword**

Synonym City

I n Synonym City, words of a feather need to stick together. Can you sort the words with identical or similar meanings into groups? Try it without using the dictionary. Part of the first puzzle is done for you as an example. Note: There may be extra blank columns for some of these puzzles.

Puzzle #1

	alibi	trace	dale	imprecation
alibi	_____	_____	_____	_____
trace	_____	_____	_____	_____
dale	_____	_____	_____	_____
imprecation	_____	_____	_____	_____
track	_____	_____	_____	_____
profanity	_____	_____	_____	_____
excuse	_____	_____	_____	_____
valley				
glen				
vestige				
blasphemy				
curse				

Puzzle #2

reproduction   _____   _____   _____   _____

prowess   _____   _____   _____   _____

capitulation   _____   _____   _____   _____

facsimile   _____   _____   _____   _____

replica   _____   _____   _____   _____

gallantry   _____   _____   _____   _____

duplicate

valor

gradation

copy

surrender

nuance

Puzzle #3

relinquish   _____   _____   _____   _____

stroll   _____   _____   _____   _____

surrender   _____   _____   _____   _____

abandon   _____   _____   _____   _____

saunter   _____   _____   _____   _____

resign   _____   _____   _____   _____

amble

mosey

scar

yield

cicatrize

waive

Puzzle #4

altitudinous   _____ _____ _____ _____

warlike   _____ _____ _____ _____

lofty   _____ _____ _____ _____

vintage   _____ _____ _____ _____

traditional   _____ _____ _____ _____

adventitious   _____ _____ _____ _____

martial

elevated

supervenient

bellicose

extraneous

classic

Puzzle #5

reprove   _____ _____ _____

deposit   _____ _____ _____

grieve   _____ _____ _____

admonish   _____ _____ _____

reproach   _____ _____ _____

cache   _____ _____ _____

bemoan

reprimand

lament

weep

bank

rebuke

Puzzle #6

inciter   _____   _____   _____

fate   _____   _____   _____

aide-de-camp   _____   _____   _____

fomenter   _____   _____   _____

coadjutant   _____   _____   _____

destiny   _____   _____   _____

lot

instigator

doom

portion

assistant

lieutenant

Puzzle #7

adventure   _____   _____   _____

outline   _____   _____   _____

morsel   _____   _____   _____

contour   _____   _____   _____

exploit   _____   _____   _____

savory   _____   _____   _____

feat

enterprise

silhouette

delicacy

tidbit

profile

Puzzle #8

habitat   _____   _____   _____

crotchet   _____   _____   _____

caprice   _____   _____   _____

locality   _____   _____   _____

wharf   _____   _____   _____

home   _____   _____   _____

haunt

whim

dock

quay

vagary

pier

Puzzle #9

slip   _____   _____   _____

lapse   _____   _____   _____

vituperation   _____   _____   _____

mistake   _____   _____   _____

triumph   _____   _____   _____

error   _____   _____   _____

billingsgate

blunder

obloquy

jubilance

exultation

invective

Puzzle #10

divert   _____   _____   _____   _____

evoke   _____   _____   _____   _____

foreordain   _____   _____   _____   _____

amuse   _____   _____   _____   _____

educe   _____   _____   _____   _____

predestine   _____   _____   _____   _____

atonement

predetermine

extract

reparation

propitiation

elicit

Classical Gas

L isted below are definitions or hints for twelve words that are built from the Greek combining forms and affixes listed at the end of this puzzle. Put together the word elements to create a word that fits the definition or hint. A few of the answers have neither a prefix nor a suffix, but are simply the combination of two combining forms. Use *Webster's Third* to confirm that you have created actual words.

1. Mr. Potato Head's numerous proboscides make it a cinch for you to perform this surgical procedure on him. Clueless? A special kind of "job" desired by Michael Jackson, among many others.

   _____

2. With this condition, a cat would have little chance getting away from a dog. _____

3. Because of this creature's "skin condition," it would be hard to hurt his feelings. _____

4. A condition in which there is wasting away because of lack of nourishment. _____

5. A condition in which there is no memory. _____

6. Without these "containers," we'd all be able to cry only crocodile tears.

   _____

7. "Madam, I'm Adam" is a well-known one of these. (It reads backward as well as forward.) _____

8. Another word for the act of drooling. _____

9. A person with this condition could never be successful if he or she lived by the motto "No pain, no gain." _____

10. A state of lawlessness. _____

11. One who maintains that he has no knowledge of a god or any ultimates. _____

12. Poor Marie Antoinette died in this state, her head in the basket.

_____

PREFIX	MEANING
a-, an-	not; without

GREEK COMBINING FORM	MEANING
onych-, onycho-	nail of the finger or toe; claw
ptyal-, ptyalo-	saliva
troph-, tropho-	nutrition
drom-, dromo-	course; running
pachy-	thick
mnem-, mnemo-	memory
dacry-, dacryo-	of a tear or tears; lacrimal
-plasty	plastic surgery
alg-, algo-	pain
rhin-, rhino-	nose
-gnosis	knowledge; cognition
nomo-	law
derm-, derma-, dermo-	skin
pali- (from Greek **palin**)	again; back
phob-, phobo-	fear; avoidance
cephal-, cephalo- (transliterated version of Greek **kephal-, kephalo-**)	head
cyst-, cysti-, cysto- (transliterated version of Greek **kyst-, kysto-**)	sac; pouch

SUFFIX	MEANING
-ia	quality, state, condition; pathological condition
-y	state, condition, quality
-ism	act, practice, process
-ic	one having the character or nature of

Magic Square

A magic square is a square of letters that reads the same across (along the rows) and down (along the columns). An example is:

C	A	L	M
A	R	I	A
L	I	A	R
M	A	R	E

In this puzzle, choose three of the combining forms shown below and use them to form a magic square.

axi-	axis	**tri-**	three	**myc-**	fungus
epi-	upon	**nas-**	nose	**mal-**	bad
xen-	guest; foreigner	**gyr-**	circle	**ino-**	fiber
pre-	earlier than	**syn-**	together	**uni-**	one

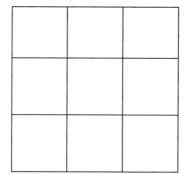

Was that too easy? Try it with a four-row square. You might think it would only be a little harder, but you may be surprised. Good luck!

zygo- yoke	**hyps-** height	**phos-** light
sten- close; narrow	**meli-** honey	**kino-** motion; action
goni- corner	**oste-** bone	**pter-** wing
cyan- dark blue	**tera-** trillion	**hist-** tissue

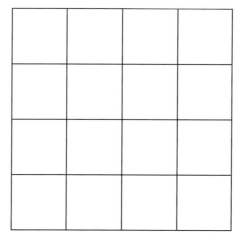

Where in the World?

Think you know a lot about geography? These forty-five words—whose meanings, figuratively speaking, are all over the map—are all derived from place names. See if you can match the word to the place its name refers to (which is not necessarily related to its language of origin!).

arcadia   An inlet between Canada and the United States
_____

assisi   Mosul, Iraq _____

attic   A region in northern France _____

axminster   A mountain in China _____

bayonet   A village in the Netherlands _____

blarney   A city in the province of Toledo, Spain _____

bougie   A river in Scotland _____

brummagem   A region of ancient Greece _____

calico   A mine in South Africa _____

castile   A large city in the English Midlands _____

chautauqua   A region of central Spain _____

cordovan   A city on the Elbe River in Germany _____

denim   A district of ancient Palestine _____

Edam   A castle near Cork, Ireland _____

glengarry   A large city of northern Morocco _____

guinea   A city in southeastern France _____

hantavirus   A former province of Japan _____

hardanger   A pastoral area of ancient Greece _____

huapango   A state in central Mexico _____

jeans	A village in western France _____
leghorn	Genoa, Italy _____
limerick	A town in the Perugia province of Italy _____
lisle	China's largest city _____
madrilene	A river in Ontario, Canada _____
magenta	A seaport in southern Italy _____
magnet	A river in South Korea _____
massasauga	A leading resort on the French Riviera _____
Meissen	A fishing village in Yucatan, Mexico _____
milliner	A port city in the Tuscany region of Italy _____
muslin	A town near Veracruz, Mexico _____
Nicoise	A city in India _____
Percheron	An ancient city in Thessaly, Greece _____
poblano	A city in southwest Ireland _____
quoddy	A region in west Africa _____
samaritan	A town in Devon, England _____
satsuma	A district in Norway _____
shanghai	A lake in western New York state _____
sisal	A town in northern Italy _____
soubise	An Algerian seaport _____
sunglo	A valley in Inverness-shire, Scotland _____
Talavera	A French city near the Belgian border _____
tangerine	A city of the French Basque area _____
tarantula	The capital city of Spain _____
tweed	A city in the Andalusian region of Spain _____
wesselton	Milan, Italy _____

Anagram Fest

An anagram is a word made by transposing the letters of another word, like **anemic** and **cinema**. Below are a number of definitions in pairs, with the number of letters given. Fill in the words and add the numbered letters to the appropriate blanks at the bottom of the puzzle. When all the letters are filled in, you'll see the name of a famous English wordsmith.

Example:

| (6 letters) | perceive with the ear | L I S T E N |
| | making no utterance | S I L E N T |

(8 letters) occurring before birth p __ __ __ __ __ __ __
                                          2

of or relating to a father p __ __ __ __ __ __ __

(5 letters) not tamed or domesticated : wild f __ __ __ __
                                                    4

flame up brightly f __ __ __ __

(7 letters) being in the state of matrimony m __ __ __ __ __ __

one who esteems or regards highly a __ __ __ __ __ __

(6 letters) more wicked e __ __ __ __ __

address or assail with opprobrious language r __ __ __ __ __
                                                15

| (5 letters) | the whole body of salt water that covers nearly three-fourths of the globe | o _ _ _ _ |
| | a long narrow boat that is sharp at both ends and has curved sides | c _ _ _ _ |

| (6 letters) | characterized by warmth or heat of emotion | a _ _ _ _ _
 11 |
| | declaimed in a bombastic fashion | r _ _ _ _ _ |

| (6 letters) | having rhythmic fall | c _ _ _ _ _ |
| | pour (as wine) from the original bottle into another container | d _ _ _ _ _ |

| (5 letters) | a person deprived of rights and privileges and often exploited | h _ _ _ _ |
| | inn | h _ _ _ _
 10 |

| (7 letters) | balcony : deck | t _ _ _ _ _ _ |
| | one who arranges food and service for a social affair | c _ _ _ _ _ _ |

| (9 letters) | one of three terms into which the academic year is divided | t _ _ _ _ _ _ _ _ |
| | persons who send a sum of money to another person | r _ _ _ _ _ _ _ _ |

(8 letters)   a writing (as a book or article)
that treats a subject   t _ _ _ _ _ _ _

most wet or stained with tears   t _ _ _ _ _ _ _

(7 letters)   the fifteenth letter of the Greek
alphabet   o _ _ _ _ _ _
                                               3

like or having the capability of
a feebleminded person   m _ _ _ _ _ _

(8 letters)   marked with stripes or lines
(as on the skin)   s _ _ _ _ _ _ _

most delayed : latest   t _ _ _ _ _ _ _

(5 letters)   one that consumes food   e _ _ _ _
                                              7

the sum of good qualities that
make character   a _ _ _ _

(8 letters)   outward manner   d _ _ _ _ _ _ _

inflamed with love   e _ _ _ _ _ _ _

(8 letters)   of, relating to, or marked by
reaction   r _ _ _ _ _ _
                                          13

given to creation   c _ _ _ _ _ _

(7 letters)   varied   d _ _ _ _ _ _

amended : improved   r _ _ _ _ _ _

(7 letters)   of or relating to any area conventionally designated as east   e _ _ _ _ _ _

closest   n _ _ _ _ _
                 14

(8 letters)   treat with medicine   m _ _ _ _ _ _ _

destroy a considerable part of   d _ _ _ _ _ _ _

(9 letters)   inflammation of an artery   a _ _ _ _ _ _ _ _

incites impatience, anger, or displeasure   i _ _ _ _ _ _ _ _

(7 letters)   forms or checks indicating a credit against a future purchase   c _ _ _ _ _ _

a little bit   s _ _ _ _ _ _

(10 letters)   a substance that prevents the growth or action of microorganisms   a _ _ _ _ _ _ _ _ _
                                                       9

of or relating to parrots of the family Psittacidae   p _ _ _ _ _ _ _ _

(8 letters)   of, relating to, or situated in Asia   o _ _ _ _ _ _ _

the act of telling or recounting   r _ _ _ _ _ _ _

(8 letters)   divided into chambers   c _ _ _ _ _ _ _

cause (solid matter) to become soft by steeping in fluid   m _ _ _ _ _ _ _

(7 letters)   a protein or carbohydrate
substance stimulating the
production of an antibody   a _ _ _ _ _ _
                                        1

a fall-blooming North American
plant having tubular blue flowers   g _ _ _ _ _ _

(9 letters)   having a high proportion of debt
relative to equity   l _ _ _ _ _ _ _ _

a swampy grassland especially
in southern Florida   e _ _ _ _ _ _ _ _

(7 letters)   of, relating to, or appropriate
to slaves   s _ _ _ _ _ _

those who impose or collect by
legal process or by authority   l _ _ _ _ _ _

(9 letters)   government in accordance
with a system of law   n _ _ _ _ _ _ _ _
                                                      8

government by a single person   m _ _ _ _ _ _ _ _

(7 letters)   freed from guilt or blame   c _ _ _ _ _ _
                                                        6

make known publicly, formally,
or explicitly   d _ _ _ _ _ _

(9 letters)   murder of a mother by her son
or daughter   m _ _ _ _ _ _ _ _

completely opposed or opposite   d _ _ _ _ _ _ _ _

(7 letters)   executed in a drawn-out manner :
sustained
s _ _ _ _ _ _
₁₂

having little substance or strength   t
_ _ _ _ _ _

(7 letters)   emotionally out of control : frenzied   f
_ _ _ _ _ _
₅

break : violate   i
_ _ _ _ _ _

_ _ _ _ _ _ _ _ _ _ _ _ _ _ _
1   2   3   4   5   6   7   8   9   10 11 12 13 14 15

Word Search:

-*able* Was I Ere I Saw -*ible*

There are twenty common words ending in -*able* and -*ible* buried in the word search puzzle below. See if you can find all of them.

divisible	excusable	exhaustible	affable
invincible	fungible	adaptable	risible
transmissible	equitable	detestable	negotiable
indelible	deductible	locatable	educable
omissible	mandible	friable	irresistible

e	q	t	r	a	n	s	m	i	s	s	i	b	l	e
a	x	e	l	b	a	t	p	a	d	a	r	i	n	e
b	a	h	e	l	b	i	t	s	i	s	e	r	r	i
l	m	o	a	f	f	a	b	l	e	s	l	b	n	n
e	a	m	i	u	r	p	p	b	l	r	b	l	e	v
e	n	i	n	n	s	i	y	l	i	e	r	e	g	i
l	d	s	d	g	y	t	a	s	l	p	l	e	o	n
b	i	s	e	i	e	t	i	b	l	e	o	l	t	c
i	b	i	l	b	l	b	a	b	l	o	c	b	i	i
t	l	b	i	l	l	c	i	b	l	e	a	a	a	b
c	e	l	b	e	u	x	i	b	l	e	t	s	b	l
u	d	e	l	d	a	s	b	l	e	t	a	u	l	e
d	e	t	e	s	t	a	b	l	e	i	b	c	e	b
e	l	b	a	t	i	u	q	e	y	b	l	x	w	l
d	i	v	i	s	i	b	l	e	m	l	e	e	p	e

Wordmeister Challenge: A Very Verbose Verbigram

These thirty-seven words are themselves all about words and language. To help you out, some of the letters have already been filled in. There are a few tough words, so remember, the dictionary is your friend! When you've found them all, the letters in the boxes, written in order, will form a quotation by the most famous Roman of all time.

Example:

a long narrative poem recounting the deeds of a legendary or historical hero

<u>e</u> <u>p</u> [i] <u>c</u>

versed in the use of language: ready with words <u>f</u> <u>☐</u> <u> </u> <u>e</u> <u> </u> <u>t</u>

a word or phrase that must be spoken by a person before he is allowed to pass a barrier or guard <u>p</u> <u> </u> <u>s</u> <u> </u> <u> </u> <u>☐</u> <u> </u> <u>d</u>

to make briefer <u>a</u> <u> </u> <u>b</u> <u> </u> <u> </u> <u>☐</u> <u> </u> <u> </u> <u> </u> <u>e</u>

the vocabulary of a language, of an individual speaker, of a set of documents, of a body of speech, or of an occupational or other group

<u>l</u> <u>☐</u> <u>x</u> <u> </u> <u> </u> <u> </u> <u>n</u>

a particular form of expression <u>l</u> <u> </u> <u>c</u> <u> </u> <u>☐</u> <u> </u> <u> </u> <u>n</u>

an untrue assertion especially when intentional

<u>f</u> <u> </u> <u> </u> <u>s</u> <u> </u> <u>☐</u> <u> </u> <u>d</u>

a transposition of usually initial sounds of two or more words that generally creates a comic effect <u>s</u> <u> </u> <u>p</u> <u> </u> <u> </u> <u> </u> <u>☐</u> <u> </u> <u> </u> <u>s</u> <u> </u> <u>m</u>

one that renders from one language or system to another

t __ __ □ __ __ __ __ o r

a tale traditional among a people and characteristically anonymous, timeless, and placeless f o __ __ __ □ __ e

a polite, tactful, or less explicit term used to avoid the direct naming of an unpleasant, painful, or frightening reality e __ __ p __ __ □ __ __ s m

marked by the brief expression of a comprehensive matter

c o __ __ □ __ d __ __ u s

the use of a new word or expression or of an established word in a new or different sense n __ □ l __ __ __ y

the characteristic language of official statements

o f □ __ __ __ __ __ __ __ s e

give the meaning of (a work or passage) in other words

p __ __ r __ __ □ __ __ s e

the science of sound

__ h □ __ i __ __ __

a formula of words chanted or recited in a magic ritual for their special virtues or particular effects i __ __ c __ □ __ __ __ __ o n

the mark (') used to indicate omission of one or more letters or figures

a p __ __ __ __ □ __ __ e

to tell or recite the happenings of (a story) n __ __ r □ __ __ e

the characteristic system or the preferred system of inflections and syntax of a language g __ __ ☐ __ __ __ r

the naming of a thing or action by a more or less exact reproduction of the sound associated with it o __ n __ o __ __ __ ☐ __ __ __ __ a __

the act or instance of stealing and passing off as one's own the ideas or words of another p __ l __ __ __ __ __ ☐ __ s __ m

a local or regional variety of language distinguished by features of vocabulary, grammar, and pronunciation from other local or regional varieties d __ __ __ ☐ c __ t

the art or practice of writing or speaking as a means of communication or persuasion often with special concern for literary effect
__ r __ h __ ☐ __ __ __ c __

to incite by argument or advice e __ x __ ☐ __ __ __ t __

any particular set of letters with which one or more languages are written
a __ __ p __ ☐ __ __ t __

the act or process or an instance of naming
n __ o __ __ ☐ __ __ __ t __ r __ e

to avoid committing oneself in what one says
e __ q __ __ ☐ __ __ __ __ t __ e

a term of address that conveys respect h __ __ n __ __ __ ☐ __ c

an ungrammatical combination of words in a sentence
s __ o __ ☐ __ __ s __ m

an often prolonged parley usually between persons of different levels of culture or sophistication p a ☐ v   r

the use of an unnecessarily large number of words to express an idea
c i ☐ c _ _ _ _ _ _ _ _ _ _ n

very long words (literally, words a foot and a half long)
s e q _ _ _ ☐ _ _ a

in a manner capable of being understood or comprehended
i t ☐ _ _ _ _ b _ y

a writing composed of words not having a certain letter
l i _ _ g _ ☐ m

able to read and write l _ ☐ _ _ _ t e

of or relating to correct spelling
o r _ ☐ g _ _ _ _ c

Quotation: _ _ _ _ _ _ _ _ _ _ _ _ _

_ _ _ _ _ _ _ _ _ _ _ _ _ _ _ _ _

_ _ _ _

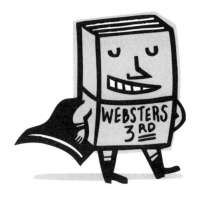

Wordmeister Super Challenge:
Greek Word Search

There are thirty English words that came from Greek hidden up, down, sideways, and diagonally in this puzzle. Check the definition to see if you can figure out the word, then find it in the grid. The word's length and first letter are given as an extra clue. Use your dictionary to help you! If you have access to the dictionary on CD-ROM, consider this a chance to practice using the search features.

r	t	c	i	c	a	r	o	h	t	i	s	o	n	o	m	y	o	s	y
n	z	d	i	c	o	s	a	h	e	d	r	o	n	c	e	r	x	i	s
a	e	w	d	y	s	p	t	b	g	r	y	l	e	a	o	o	y	s	k
x	r	o	s	e	p	o	i	l	l	a	c	n	b	o	m	l	l	o	r
e	s	t	p	m	d	l	m	i	m	e	t	i	c	i	s	o	e	b	y
m	r	s	n	h	i	b	a	g	d	t	y	i	n	o	i	c	m	m	p
u	u	c	a	o	y	b	r	h	r	v	r	x	a	z	m	e	y	o	t
m	n	i	u	n	r	t	r	e	t	e	c	a	r	d	e	t	t	r	o
e	p	n	t	y	m	c	e	u	m	n	h	l	i	t	h	i	c	h	n
h	s	e	i	s	o	x	u	o	x	y	e	d	z	l	p	c	e	t	u
t	r	h	l	a	m	p	h	i	b	i	o	u	s	o	u	l	v	t	s
n	l	t	u	s	c	i	r	r	e	l	l	k	i	v	e	x	a	d	s
a	o	s	s	g	h	r	q	l	d	h	i	m	g	c	w	e	n	r	a
s	g	i	c	a	r	e	o	w	n	p	n	r	t	n	o	r	g	d	i
y	o	l	n	d	e	t	b	p	z	a	x	r	y	l	x	o	e	m	n
r	m	a	v	m	s	p	x	t	o	t	o	m	p	b	u	s	l	c	o
h	a	c	o	y	a	h	r	c	u	l	i	r	h	y	n	i	i	g	n
c	c	y	s	e	r	y	n	r	y	y	i	d	u	e	r	s	z	t	i
t	h	n	a	t	d	s	o	t	d	i	o	s	s	o	l	g	e	m	o
m	y	r	i	a	d	e	e	p	s	t	a	l	a	g	m	i	t	e	k

1. the upper fortified part of an ancient Greek city (9)

   a _ _ _ _ _ _ _ _

2. able to live both on land and in water (10)

   a _ _ _ _ _ _ _ _ _

3. the habit of unconsciously gritting or grinding the teeth, especially in situations of stress or during sleep (7) b _ _ _ _ _ _

4. systematic exercises performed usually in rhythm and often in a group without apparatus or with light hand apparatus to improve the strength, suppleness, balance, and health of the body (12)

   c _ _ _ _ _ _ _ _ _ _ _

5. a musical instrument consisting of a series of crude steam or air whistles used on riverboats and in circuses and carnivals (8)

   c _ _ _ _ _ _ _

6. the soil water available for plant growth (8) c _ _ _ _ _ _ _

7. a large genus of perennial herbs that are widely distributed in the Old World and that include many plants derived chiefly from two species, which are probably Asiatic though known only in cultivation and are cultivated for their showy often double and brightly colored flower heads (13) c _ _ _ _ _ _ _ _ _ _ _ _

8. a substance (as an acid, base, or salt) that when dissolved in a suitable solvent (as water) or when fused becomes an ionic conductor (11)

   e _ _ _ _ _ _ _ _ _ _

9. a thermodynamic quantity that is the sum of the internal energy of a body and the product of its volume multiplied by the pressure (8)

   e _ _ _ _ _ _ _

10. the substitution of an agreeable or inoffensive word or expression for one that is harsh, indelicate, or otherwise unpleasant or taboo (9)

    e _ _ _ _ _ _ _ _

11. to preach the gospel (10) e _ _ _ _ _ _ _ _ _

12. resembling a tongue (8) g _ _ _ _ _ _ _

13. of or relating to the Greek poet Homer, his age, or his writings (7)
    H _ _ _ _ _ _

14. a polyhedron having twenty faces (11) i _ _ _ _ _ _ _ _ _ _

15. equality before the law (7) i _ _ _ _ _ _

16. intimate spiritual communion and participative sharing in a common
    religious commitment and spiritual community (8)
    k _ _ _ _ _ _ _

17. a colorless inert gaseous element that occurs in air to the extent of
    about one part per million by volume and in gases from thermal springs
    and other natural gases, that is obtained by separating from liquid air,
    and that is used in electric lamps (7) k _ _ _ _ _ _

18. of or relating to stone (6) l _ _ _ _ _

19. a dispute over or about words (9) l _ _ _ _ _ _ _ _

20. having an aptitude for or a tendency toward mimicry (7)
    m _ _ _ _ _ _

21. an immense number (6) m _ _ _ _ _

22. any of several cephalopod mollusks of the southern Pacific and Indian
    oceans that constitute a genus and that are contained in the outermost
    chamber of a spiral chambered shell with an outer porcelaneous layer
    and an inner pearly layer (8) n _ _ _ _ _ _ _

23. a young or inexperienced practitioner or student (8)
    n _ _ _ _ _ _ _

24. a deposit of crystalline calcium carbonate, more or less like an inverted
    stalactite, formed on the floor of a cave by the drip of water saturated

with calcium bicarbonate and often uniting with a stalactite in a complete column (10) s _ _ _ _ _ _ _ _ _

25. the contraction of the heart by which the blood is forced onward and the circulation kept up (7) s _ _ _ _ _ _

26. of, relating to, located within, or involving the thorax (8)
    t _ _ _ _ _ _ _

27. the formation or presence of a blood clot within a blood vessel (10)
    t _ _ _ _ _ _ _ _ _

28. a severe febrile disease characterized by high fever, stupor alternating with delirium, intense headache, and a dark red rash and caused by a rickettsia (*Rickettsia prowazekii*) that is transmitted especially by body lice (6) t _ _ _ _ _

29. abnormal dryness of a body part or tissue (as the skin or conjunctiva) (7) x _ _ _ _ _ _

30. a complex tissue in the vascular system of higher plants typically constituting the woody element (5) x _ _ _ _

Wordmeister Super Challenge:
French Word Search

There are forty English words that came from French hidden up, down, sideways, and diagonally in this puzzle. Check the definition to see if you can figure out the word, then find it in the grid. The word's length and first letter are given as an extra clue. Use your dictionary to help you! If you have access to the dictionary on CD-ROM, consider this a chance to practice using the search features.

e	t	o	c	s	i	n	q	u	e	s	p	l	a	n	a	d	e	i	r
l	u	p	o	p	i	e	w	n	p	a	e	n	o	t	o	l	e	p	s
v	t	p	e	g	a	l	e	s	u	f	n	i	l	e	n	y	u	j	h
a	p	o	r	l	r	l	t	t	a	j	l	t	c	i	f	j	g	l	a
u	m	u	n	t	i	j	t	r	t	h	a	a	a	h	u	f	i	o	u
d	o	s	r	r	p	u	e	o	v	e	i	r	n	h	e	b	a	r	t
e	r	e	d	n	e	l	u	p	y	v	g	a	m	e	l	a	n	g	e
v	p	a	j	u	k	i	q	p	z	s	e	f	t	n	u	i	r	n	u
i	m	v	t	a	f	e	o	a	o	z	o	u	a	v	e	r	r	e	r
l	i	a	e	q	u	n	c	r	o	u	p	i	e	r	e	u	k	t	f
l	o	l	i	z	a	n	g	a	y	n	r	e	u	e	u	q	l	t	c
e	r	u	k	l	m	e	a	m	u	e	i	v	o	q	e	u	e	e	l
a	m	m	n	c	l	r	i	u	v	n	o	i	j	e	t	a	f	h	y
v	o	i	o	n	t	o	i	r	b	i	v	l	e	p	t	t	v	c	e
r	l	n	h	i	h	e	t	i	b	a	e	n	r	a	e	o	i	i	u
i	u	a	c	l	l	n	v	a	f	r	d	a	v	t	s	r	e	u	a
l	m	i	o	e	a	o	u	o	r	e	n	e	u	o	i	z	r	q	e
t	i	r	b	v	u	m	o	d	i	s	t	e	e	i	o	a	e	t	d
e	l	e	a	a	r	e	c	n	a	i	c	u	o	s	n	i	s	s	i
r	i	s	c	j	t	o	l	c	l	i	m	o	u	s	i	n	e	v	r

1. a song or poem greeting the dawn (6) a _ _ _ _ _

2. an encampment under little or no shelter usually for a short time (7)
   b _ _ _ _ _ _

3. an uncut gem somewhat polished (8) c _ _ _ _ _ _ _

4. a woman who endeavors without affection to attract men's amorous attention (8) c _ _ _ _ _ _ _

5. a representative of a gambling house or casino who officiates at a gaming table (8) c _ _ _ _ _ _ _

6. an act or conduct that may be required or expected of one (6)
   d _ _ _ _ _

7. a level open stretch of paved or grassy ground (9)
   e _ _ _ _ _ _ _ _

8. an aimless and usually self-centered and superficial person (7)
   f _ _ _ _ _ _

9. the central body portion of an airplane designed to accommodate the crew and the passengers or cargo (8) f _ _ _ _ _ _ _

10. a marked, especially social or diplomatic, blunder or clumsy mistake (5)
    g _ _ _ _

11. a firm fabric in plain weave usually of silk or rayon and a heavy cotton filling that forms pronounced crosswise ribs (9)
    g _ _ _ _ _ _ _ _

12. arrogant or condescending manner (7)
    h _ _ _ _ _ _

13. made, done, or formed on or as if on the spur of the moment (9)
    i _ _ _ _ _ _ _ _

14. freedom from concern or care (11) i _ _ _ _ _ _ _ _ _ _

15. a slender shaft of wood not less than 260 centimeters long, tipped with iron or steel, and intended to be thrown for distance as an athletic feat or exercise (7) j _ _ _ _ _ _

16. cut in long thin strips—used especially of vegetables and fruit (8)
    j _ _ _ _ _ _ _

17. a military cap having a close-fitting band, a round flat top sloping toward the front, and a visor (4) k _ _ _

18. a large luxurious sedan, especially one for hire and seating five persons behind the driver (9) l _ _ _ _ _ _ _ _

19. a pair of eyeglasses or opera glasses with a handle (9)
    l _ _ _ _ _ _ _ _

20. a complete lighting unit including lamp, shade, reflector, fixture, and other accessories (9) l _ _ _ _ _ _ _ _

21. a consommé flavored with tomato and served hot or cold (9)
    m _ _ _ _ _ _ _ _

22. a woman's one-piece, usually strapless, bathing suit (7)
    m _ _ _ _ _ _

23. a mixture of heterogeneous and often incongruous elements (7)
    m _ _ _ _ _ _

24. one who makes and sells fashionable dresses and hats for women (7)
    m _ _ _ _ _ _

25. a small piece of lean meat (as the eye of a chop or a small slice of tenderloin) (8) n _ _ _ _ _ _ _

26. a substantial body of work constituting the lifework of a writer, an artist, or a composer (6) o _ _ _ _ _

27. a brass made to imitate gold and used in mounts for furniture and for other decorative purposes (6) o _ _ _ _ _

28. a dialect other than the standard or literary dialect (6)
   p _ _ _ _ _

29. the main body of riders in a bicycle race (7) p _ _ _ _ _ _

30. a poem resembling a sonnet but lacking strict sonnet structure (10)
   q _ _ _ _ _ _ _ _ _

31. to line up or wait in a line especially of persons or vehicles (5)
   q _ _ _ _

32. a baked custard pie usually having an added savory ingredient (as chopped ham, seafood, or vegetables) (6) q _ _ _ _ _

33. relation characterized by harmony, conformity, accord, or affinity (7)
   r _ _ _ _ _ _

34. a small ridge or mound of earth (6) r _ _ _ _ _

35. a person with detailed knowledge in some specialized field (as of science or literature) (6) s _ _ _ _ _

36. an oscillation of the surface of a lake or landlocked sea that varies in period from a few minutes to several hours (6) s _ _ _ _ _

37. a brownish gray that is paler and slightly yellower than chocolate, duller and slightly redder than mouse gray, and duller and slightly redder than castor (5) t _ _ _ _

38. an alarm bell or the ringing of a bell for the purpose of alarm (6)
   t _ _ _ _ _

39. a stage entertainment especially popular in theaters in the early decades of the twentieth century that consisted of various unrelated acts following one another in succession (10) v _ _ _ _ _ _ _ _ _

40. one of a body of French infantry originally composed of Algerians that is characterized by a colorful uniform and by a very quick and spirited drill (6) z _ _ _ _ _

Chapter 7 Answer Key

Add Diction

1. sin sing using busing abusing
2. ion lion legion legation allegation
3. ail nail snail snakily snarkily
4. hog Hong hoping hopping shopping
5. did died dived divided dividend
6. lie lite liter lister blister
7. rob robe probe probate probative
8. and sand stand strand stranded
9. rue rube ruble rumble crumble
10. ace lace lance valance avalanche

Dictionary Devil

1. angstrom: a unit of length equal to one ten-billionth of a meter
   baccarat: a card game played especially in European casinos
   pegasus: a fabulous winged horse
   homily: an unusually short sermon
   quadruped: an animal having four feet
   picayune: something trivial
   plaint: lamentation, wail
   bravura: a show of daring or brilliance

2. crenation: one of the rounded projections on an edge (as of a coin)
   funicular: a cable railway ascending a mountain
   loge: a small compartment
   marquetry: inlaid work of wood, shell, or ivory (as on a table or cabinet)
   macle: a twinned crystal
   odyssey: a long wandering marked usually by many changes of fortune

quarto: the size of a piece of paper cut four from a sheet

whippet: any of a breed of small swift slender dogs that are used for racing

3. audit: a methodical examination and review

vesicant: an agent that causes blistering

zinger: a pointed witty remark

acknowledgment: a thing done or given in recognition of something received

depot: storehouse

angst: a feeling of anxiety, apprehension, or insecurity

mousse: a foamy preparation used in styling hair

pinto: a spotted horse or pony

4. abjection: a low or downcast state

peer: one that is of equal standing with another

festoon: a decorative chain or strip hanging between two points

pseudonym: a fictitious name

remuda: the herd of horses from which those to be used for the day are chosen

seine: a large weighted fishing net

bifurcation: separation or branching into two parts or connected segments

whelp: any of the young of various carnivorous mammals (as a dog)

5. firebrand: agitator

tundra: a treeless plain of arctic and subarctic regions

visage: the face or countenance of a person or sometimes an animal

question: an interrogative sentence or clause

mithridate: an antidote against poison

butte: an isolated steep hill

cygnet: a young swan

rhapsodist: a professional reciter of epic poems

6. unabridged: being the most complete of its class
   deprecatory: seeking to avert approval
   superlative: of very high quality
   edentulous: toothless
   eloquent: vividly or movingly expressive or revealing
   synthetic: produced artificially
   cynical: contemptuously distrustful of human nature and motives
   fanatic: marked by excessive enthusiasm and often intense
      uncritical devotion

7. pastiche: a composition made of selections from different works
   debutante: a young woman making her formal entrance into society
   plaiting: the interlacing of strands
   raucous: disagreeably harsh or strident
   ostrich: a very large swift-footed flightless bird of Africa and Arabia
   vim: robust energy and enthusiasm
   kokanee: a small landlocked sockeye salmon
   baronet: a man holding a rank of honor below a baron but above
      a knight

8. trilby: a soft felt hat with indented crown
   christie: a skiing turn used for altering the direction of hill descent
   populace: the common people
   vermicelli: pasta made in long solid strings smaller in diameter
      than spaghetti
   proclivity: an inclination or tendency toward something
   boudoir: a woman's dressing room, bedroom, or private sitting room
   fatback: the strip of fat from the back of a hog cured by drying and
      salting
   verdigris: a green or bluish deposit that forms on copper, brass,
      or bronze

9. kudu: a grayish brown African antelope with large spirally twisted horns

tendency: a proneness to a particular kind of thought or action

gourmand: one who is excessively fond of eating and drinking

gaff: a spear used to take fish or turtles

badinage: playful repartee

apocalypse: a writing prophesying a cataclysm in which evil forces are destroyed

tome: a large or scholarly book

vinaigrette: a sauce made typically of oil, vinegar, and seasonings

10. tirade: a prolonged speech of abuse or condemnation

biotite: a dark mica containing iron, magnesium, potassium, and aluminum

saber: a cavalry sword with a curved blade and thick back

warlock: a man practicing the black arts

affenpinscher: any of a breed of small dogs with a wiry black, red, tan, or gray coat

carabid: ground beetle

sapphire: a dark purplish-blue color

bedlam: a place, scene, or state of uproar and confusion

Synonym City

1. alibi
   excuse

   trace
   track
   vestige

   dale
   valley
   glen

   imprecation
   profanity
   blasphemy
   curse

2. reproduction
   facsimile
   replica
   copy
   duplicate

   prowess
   gallantry
   valor

   capitulation
   surrender

   gradation
   nuance

3. relinquish   stroll   scar
   surrender   saunter   cicatrize
   abandon   amble
   resign   mosey
   waive
   yield

4. altitudinous   warlike   vintage   adventitious
   lofty   martial   traditional   supervenient
   elevated   bellicose   classic   extraneous

5. reprove   deposit   grieve
   admonish   cache   bemoan
   reproach   bank   lament
   reprimand   weep
   rebuke

6. inciter   fate   aide-de-camp
   fomenter   destiny   coadjutant
   instigator   lot   assistant
     doom   lieutenant
     portion

7. adventure   outline   morsel
   exploit   contour   savory
   feat   silhouette   delicacy
   enterprise   profile   tidbit

8. habitat   crotchet   wharf
   locality   caprice   dock
   home   whim   quay
   haunt   vagary   pier

9. slip   vituperation   triumph
    lapse   billingsgate   jubilance
    mistake   obloquy   exultation
    error   invective
    blunder

10. divert   evoke   foreordain   atonement
    amuse   educe   predestine   reparation
        extract   predetermine   propitiation
        elicit

Classical Gas

1. rhinoplasty

2. anonychia

3. pachyderm

4. atrophy

5. amnesia

6. dacryocyst

7. palindrome

8. ptyalism

9. algophobia, analgesia

10. anomie, anomia, anomy

11. agnostic

12. acephalous

Magic Square

A	X	I
X	E	N
I	N	O

P	H	O	S
H	I	S	T
O	S	T	E
S	T	E	N

Where in the World?

arcadia	A pastoral area of ancient Greece
assisi	A town in the Perugia province of Italy
attic	A region of ancient Greece
axminster	A town in Devon, England
bayonet	A city of the French Basque area
blarney	A castle near Cork, Ireland
bougie	An Algerian seaport
brummagem	A large city in the English Midlands
calico	A city in India
castile	A region of central Spain
chautauqua	A lake in western New York state
cordovan	A city in the Andalusian region of Spain
denim	A city in southeastern France
Edam	A village in the Netherlands
glengarry	A valley in Inverness-shire, Scotland

guinea	A region in west Africa
hantavirus	A river in South Korea
hardanger	A district in Norway
huapango	A town near Veracruz, Mexico
jeans	Genoa, Italy
leghorn	A port city in the Tuscany region of Italy
limerick	A city in southwest Ireland
lisle	A French city near the Belgian border
madrilene	The capital city of Spain
magenta	A town in northern Italy
magnet	An ancient city in Thessaly, Greece
massasauga	A river in Ontario, Canada
Meissen	A city on the Elbe River in Germany
milliner	Milan, Italy
muslin	Mosul, Iraq
Nicoise	A leading resort on the French Riviera
Percheron	A region in northern France
poblano	A state in central Mexico
quoddy	An inlet between Canada and the United States
samaritan	A district of ancient Palestine
satsuma	A former province of Japan
shanghai	China's largest city
sisal	A fishing village in Yucatan, Mexico
soubise	A village in western France
sunglo	A mountain in China
Talavera	A city in the province of Toledo, Spain
tangerine	A large city of northern Morocco
tarantula	A seaport in southern Italy
tweed	A river in Scotland
wesselton	A mine in South Africa

Anagram Fest

prenatal/paternal

feral/flare

married/admirer

eviler/revile

ocean/canoe

ardent/ranted

cadent/decant

helot/hotel

terrace/caterer

trimester/remitters

treatise/teariest

omicron/moronic

striated/tardiest

eater/arete

demeanor/enamored

reactive/creative

diverse/revised

eastern/nearest

medicate/decimate

arteritis/irritates

coupons/soupcon

antiseptic/psittacine

oriental/relation

camerate/macerate

antigen/gentian

leveraged/everglade

servile/leviers

nomocracy/monocracy

cleared/declare

matricide/diametric

soutenu/tenuous

frantic/infract

Answer: Geoffrey Chaucer

Word Search: -*able* Was I Ere I Saw -*ible*

e		t	r	a	n	s	m	i	s	s	i	b	l	e
	x	e	l	b	a	t	p	a	d	a				
		h	e	l	b	i	t	s	i	s	e	r	r	i
	m	o	a	f	f	a	b	l	e			n	n	
	a	m	i	u	r			r			e	v		
e	n	i	n	n	s	i		i	e			g	i	
l	d	s	d	g		t	a	s	l		l	e	o	n
b	i	s	e	i		i	b			o	l	t	c	
i	b	i	l	b		b	a	b	l		c	b	i	i
t	l	b	i	l	l	c			l	e	a	a	a	b
c	e	l	b	e	u				e	t	s	b	l	
u		e	l	d						a	u	l	e	
d	e	t	e	s	t	a	b	l	e		b	c	e	
e	l	b	a	t	i	u	q	e		l	x			
d	i	v	i	s	i	b	l	e		e	e			

Wordmeister Challenge: A Very Verbose Verbigram

epic	grammar
fluent	onomatopoeia
password	plagiarism
abbreviate	dialect
lexicon	rhetoric
locution	exhort
falsehood	alphabet
spoonerism	nomenclature
translator	equivocate
folktale	honorific
euphemism	solecism
compendious	palaver
neology	circumlocution
officialese	sesquipedalia
paraphrase	intelligibly
phonics	lipogram
incantation	literate
apostrophe	orthographic
narrate	

"I love the name of honor more than I fear death." —Julius Caesar

Wordmeister Super Challenge: Greek Word Search

acropolis	enthalpy	krypton	systole
amphibious	euphemism	lithic	thoracic
bruxism	evangelize	logomachy	thrombosis
calisthenics	glossoid	mimetic	typhus
calliope	Homeric	myriad	xerosis
chresard	icosahedron	nautilus	xylem
chrysanthemum	isonomy	neophyte	
electrolyte	koinonia	stalagmite	

		c	i	c	a	r	o	h	t	i	s	o	n	o	m	y		s	
n		i	c	o	s	a	h	e	d	r	o	n					x	i	
	e		y														y	s	k
	o		e	p	o	i	l	l	a	c					m		l	o	r
		p		l	m	i	m	e	t	i	c				s		e	b	y
m		s	n	h			a				i		i				m	m	p
u		c	a		y	b		h				r				m		o	t
m		i	u		t	r		t	e							m		r	o
e		n	t				e	u	m	n		l	i	t	h	i	c	h	n
h		e	i				o	x		e					p		e	t	
t		h	l	a	m	p	h	i	b	i	o	u	s		u	l	v		
n	l	t	u		c				e		s				e	x	a		
a	o	s	s		h	r		l				m		c		e	n		a
s	g	i			r		o						t			r	g		i
y	o	l			e	t		p				r	y			o	e		n
r	m	a			s					o		o		p		s	l		o
h	a	c		y	a			l				h				i	i		n
c	c		s		r				y			i		u		s	z		i
	h			d		t	d	i	o	s	s	o	l	g	e				o
m	y	r	i	a	d		e		s	t	a	l	a	g	m	i	t	e	k

Wordmeister Super Challenge: French Word Search

aubade	fuselage	kepi	noisette	rapport
bivouac	gaffe	limousine	oeuvre	rideau
cabochon	grosgrain	lorgnette	ormolu	savant
coquette	hauteur	luminaire	patois	seiche
croupier	impromptu	madrilene	peloton	taupe
devoir	insouciance	maillot	quatorzain	tocsin
esplanade	javelin	mélange	queue	vaudeville
flaneur	julienne	modiste	quiche	zouave

	t	o	c	s	i	n		e	s	p	l	a	n	a	d	e		
	u						n	p		e	n	o	t	o	l	e	p	
v	t		e	g	a	l	e	s	u	f		i		e	n			h
a	p				l	t	t	a		l		c	i	f			l	a
u	m			i	j	t	r	t			a	a	h		f		o	u
d	o			r	p	u	e	o			r	n		e		a	r	t
e	r		d		e	l	u	p		g		m	e	l	a	n	g	e
v	p	a			k	i	q	p		s				u			n	u
i	m				e	o	a	o	z	o	u	a	v	e	r		e	r
l	i	a				n	c	r	o	u	p	i	e	r			t	
l	o	l	i			n	g			r	e	u	e	u	q		t	
e	r	u		l		e	a			i			e	u		e		
	m	m	n		l			u			o			t	a		h	
	o	i	o	n		o		b		v		e	p	t	t		c	
	l	n	h	i			t	i		a	e		r	a	e	o		i	u
	u	a	c	l		n	v			d		v	t	s	r		u	a
		i	o	e	a	o					e	u	o	i	z		q	e
		r	b	v	u	m	o	d	i	s	t	e	e	i	o	a		d
		e	a	a		e	c	n	a	i	c	u	o	s	n	i		i
		s	c	j				l	i	m	o	u	s	i	n	e		r

Notes

Barrie Trinkle has served on the Scripps National Spelling Bee's word panel since 1997. She was the 1973 National Spelling Bee Champion (her word was *vouchsafe*).

Carolyn Andrews is the word list manager for the Scripps National Spelling Bee. Her son, Ned, was the 1994 National Spelling Bee Champion (his word was *antediluvian*).

Paige Kimble is the director of the Scripps National Spelling Bee. She was the 1981 National Spelling Bee Champion (her word was *sarcophagus*).